Lette
The
Cupboard...
by Sharon Bill

CW00482225

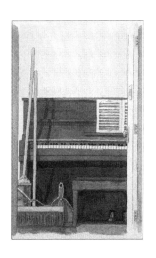

Letters From The Broom Cupboard

by Sharon Bill

www.SharonBill.com

Copyright © 2017 Sharon Bill All rights reserved.

Cover Illustration by Billy

www.BillyArt.co.uk

© Billy 2017

No portion of this book may be reproduced in any form without permission from the publisher.

To Mae,

In grateful acknowledgement of the legacy.

Author's note.

While the roots of this literary offering are firmly established in fact, the reader would do well to bear in mind that the budding offshoots have been liberally sprinkled with fairy dust.

Dear Reader,

Twenty minutes can seem an interminably long time, especially when enclosed in a windowless box-room which closely resembles a sauna. It can't be officially termed a sauna as a collection of brooms in one corner, a stack of prefabricated shelving leaning against a wall and a piano positioned against the far wall precludes the room being let for therapeutic purposes. Somebody is missing out on a significant income stream. If they only cleared the room out and placed piles of soft, fluffy towels along the aforementioned prefabricated shelves (once erected) they'd be onto a winner. I suppose it could cause some embarrassment when, in about twenty minutes time, the next pupil arrives expecting a piano lesson - if they arrive... I've completed what paperwork I can, I've had a run up and down some of scales for my own benefit and the only thing remaining to me to occupy the time and take my mind off the stifling heat is to write to you, dear reader.

There's a double-edged irony to this situation. Last year the school was undergoing 'improvements' and there was no heating whatsoever. I was clad in so many layers that, although I'm not as slim as I once was, my form was unrecognisable as human - let alone female. More significantly, twenty-five years ago I was a student at this very school and I was the errant pupil who had forgotten to attend her piano lesson - again. I'm suffering from a severe case of poetic justice.

On the other hand, twenty minutes can fly by with alarming rapidity: warm-up with a few scales and arpeggios, recap music from the previous lesson, look ahead to new material and techniques, chat about the composer or relevant musical features then play through the next piece. Before you've got to the double bar line there's somebody else knocking on the door for their lesson. (If I'm lucky).

Wherever I'm teaching - no matter how long I've been teaching each pupil - I still always get a bout of 'nerves' before I start and find that I keep nipping to the loo before there's that knock on the door. Maybe this time I'll get found out and suddenly find that I can't teach piano at all. In fact, what is a piano? Even after decades of teaching it's still the same. How ridiculous! I suppose it's because every lesson is unpredictable and is widely different from the last. I may plan ahead but there's no guarantee that's what will actually happen. The other day I was surprised to find that Pinocchio had arrived for his piano lesson. Once I'd remembered that it was World Book Day I was more prepared to find Cinderella waiting to be seated at the piano later that evening, although the costumes added a new element of chaos. Pinocchio's puppet strings kept getting caught between the piano keys. We did try and pull on them to see if they could direct him to the right notes (we really did), but to no avail. When this failed I stoically tucked the strings up his sleeves and let nature take its course. This seemed a more professional approach - surely it's better for a pupil to tie their own fingers in knots than for their tutor to do so for them by means of puppet strings.

Gratefully yours, x

Dear Reader,

Have you ever noticed what strange expressions people adopt when they're playing the piano? Of course, I've never actually seen myself playing, but I'm sure that my face remains looking eminently sensible. Every week, for half an hour solid, little Matthew sits with his tongue stuck out of the side of his mouth in a stereotypical attitude of concentration. I would worry that the aforementioned muscle would dry out and the poor lad would suffer from dehydration but, fortunately, any deleterious effects are countered by the fact that he has a constantly running nose. I spend a feverish half hour dishing out tissues aiming to prevent a transferral of fluid from nose - to hand - to keyboard. He needs that liquid for his tongue!

In general, various forms of lip twitching are the order of the day. Either that, or a vacant open-mouthed expression fits the bill. A theatrical friend of mine observed that it is simply impossible to apply eyeliner if you keep your mouth shut. Here is scientific proof that the brain and the mouth remain connected even when speech isn't involved.

However, it doesn't necessarily follow that the function of speech is disconnected when playing the piano. There is a certain type of student that can't refrain from providing a running commentary.

'Oh, yes. I remember - now I press this one."

(No response from me.)

'Then I press this one. Oh, no. Silly me! It's this one.'

(Still no response from me.)

'Is it this one now? Is this the right one?'

(Response now unavoidable.)

Dear old Mrs Simpkins took this technique to a whole new level as she was prone to stop mid-bar and launch into graphic descriptions of Mr Simpkins' trouble with piles. Keen to ensure that the old dear got musical value for money I would merely nod sagely and suggest that we try to finish playing "Over the Hills and through the Dales" despite such domestic tribulation.

I'm told that when I play I look utterly devoid of expression and convey an absolute blank of emotion. This doesn't bode well for a very inspiring performance but I can assure you, dear reader, that all of the emotion necessary for a convincing performance is projected from the depth of my inner being directly to my fingertips and so needs go nowhere near my face. My colleague's performance persona is one of absolute tranquility. It really is quite humbling to sit next to her angelic face as her fingers flutter over the keyboard. It almost makes me weep to think of the Madonna-type attitude she portrays as her beautiful spirit channels the music through to the piano's keys. I've decided that I'm going to move my piano in front of a mirror and, instead of practising the music, I'm going to practise presenting the artistic image of an acclaimed performer. Flautists are encouraged to practise in front of a mirror to correct their posture and it's only right that I follow their example. Instead of correcting drooping shoulders and elbows I shall endeavour to correct a drooping mouth.

Gratefully yours, x

Dear Reader,

I feel like we're really getting to know each other. I find myself looking forward to our brief snatches of time together. As such, it's only right and proper that I introduce you to some of my pupils. Before I begin it's perhaps necessary to point out that, although the lens which I use to capture them is less than rose tinted, I have a genuine regard for all of my pupils. For a start they share with me the desire to play music so that makes them "all right" in my book. I've never been very good at separating business from pleasure and I now count many of my pupils, both past and present, as my friends. Some of the adult pupils have seen my family grow up over the years. Terry began taking lessons when he was Forty and week by week he has seen my children grow from young childhood into their twenties. It's not unusual for them all to meet in the local pub and join each other over a friendly pint now. We attend each other's milestone birthday parties and sometimes I have to delay getting to the piano because Terry's wandered off into the garage to see my daughter's new motorbike. Either that or he's lingering in the kitchen chatting away to my husband.

Sitting side by side next to the piano week after week is bound to result in some sort of camaraderie and I can sometimes inadvertently take the place of counsellor-cum-confessor. It's not been unknown for me to abandon a lesson entirely and forego my fee. Dear Caroline arrives for her lesson each week in a state of mental exhaustion. She spends every other minute during the rest of the week caring for elderly relatives and grandchildren. There's no doubt that her family is really taking the biscuit and they need to shoulder their own responsibilities, but she's such a generous soul. One week I could see the tears welling up in her eyes so I took her into the lounge and gave her a cup of tea. There really was no point in trying to work. She came to my Fortieth birthday garden party and we keep in touch, even though she has given up lessons for the time being (practise time was always an issue). In fact it's Caroline's fault that we have our dog. Our children's friend bought her Bichon/Poodle cross over for the day because he was looking for a new home. I went into the lounge where Caroline was waiting for her lesson and she was doting over the doggy. Behind my back she was winking at the kids and she somehow wangled it so that the dog stayed with us from then on. I've always wondered how it was that she coincidentally had a spare dog basket and a bag of dog food in the boot of her car just at that time.

I read once, in a career's option guide booklet, that a private music tutor can often become a role model and mentor to their pupils. Mae (my friend and fellow music tutor) and I fell about laughing when we read this, but it's sobering to think that it mightn't be so far from the truth. It's rather poignant when you consider that my aforementioned friend was in fact my piano teacher when I was seventeen. She's also the reason I've been a member of our local choir for the last twenty-odd years (discounting breaks for raising kids). I remember singing in a Christmas concert all those years ago. As second sopranos we were on the top tier of the staging in a huge concert hall. I was full term pregnant with twins, standing high up and right next to the pipe organ that her husband was playing full pelt. At that moment I think that she was really regretting encouraging me to audition to join and she spent the whole evening on stand-by, should I suddenly become overcome with labour pains. The uniform at that time was a truly awful dress with some form of atrocious cape configuration at the front. Suffice to say that it was the only garment I could wear where it was impossible to see that I was carrying two large babies. Thank goodness the committee finally gave in to accepting simple black top and trousers as our official garb! Even then we had a fight on our hands to reign in some darling's overwhelming desire to add flouncy scarves or some such atrocity.

The chain of influence continues and it's unnerving to notice impressionable teenage girls copy my style of dress (not the height of couture) and mannerisms (not the epitome of grace). The most alarming example was when, in a flare up of mid-life crisis, I had my nose pierced. Imagine my horror when my lovely seventeen year old student came to her next lesson similarly branded. I'm trusting that this was mere coincidence as she has her very own style and her hair has been subjected to various hues of blue and green. Mind you, I had the tips of my hair coloured blue for a time. I wonder, who is influencing whom?

Gratefully yours, x

Dear Reader,

So many factors can interfere with the flow of a lesson (presuming that a pupil actually does turn up) but it's the unseen forces that create the real havoc. Non-uniform days inflict a disruptive element. It must be because wearing out of school clothes creates a holiday atmosphere and so the brain assumes that it must actually be a holiday and therefore shuts off completely. If it's a themed non-uniform day, such as World Book Day or Red Nose Day, the brain switches to party mode and rather than merely switching off becomes positively frenzied. Instead of merely becoming unable to function or think it cannot sit still and transfers its agitation to its host's bottom and limbs. In extreme cases I find it best to abandon all hope and swap places at the piano with the victim. I'll play a piece hoping that the student will follow the music and point to strategic places when I stop. Either that or I'll play some music to match their costume (if I can) where we "follow the music" and sing our hearts out.

Aspects of natural force create the most havoc and then I'm merely a pawn at the mercy of the whim of nature. If there's an unexpected burst of sunshine after a prolonged bout of dreary weather, the holiday atmosphere hits both myself and my pupils alike. We may well begin with the intention of regular work but a mood of joviality soon prevails and we find ourselves playing musical chairs as I take the piano stool to knock out some jolly tunes for the student to follow and sing along to. An extremely windy day has the same effect on concentration as a themed non-uniform day and similar strategies need to be adopted in the end. I reassure myself by pointing out (to myself, nobody else seems to care) that it's still music related and it's still educational - in a lateral sense. Sometimes it's good to take a step back from a railroad approach to teaching. Surely, to inspire a little enthusiasm is no bad thing!

There is another type of wind which has far more reaching consequences from my point of view. The time of day that lessons take place can be critical in this respect. If I teach at school in the morning it's usually risk free, but if I teach after lunch time or at home after early tea sometimes the results can be disastrous. It transpires that a child's digestive system is a finely tuned mechanism and once the meal has begun to be properly transformed into the necessary nutrients there can be no curtailing the side effects. Gregory Findley is the worst culprit. Everything about Gregory is highly sensitive and on a knife edge. His intestines must pay the price. You must understand that working one-to-one, in close proximity and in an enclosed space (namely the Broom Cupboard) alarmingly exacerbates the nuclear fall out rate. I know that you feel my pain, dear reader. Being so "Jolly British" only compounds the problem. Do I carry on regardless and pretend I haven't noticed? For all they know I could have lost my sense of smell at birth. Do I make a joke to lighten the atmosphere? (Metaphorically speaking.) I'm afraid that I'm far too British to do that with aplomb. In the worst cases I move "station" and sit the child at a desk, as far removed from the piano as possible, and write out some note revision exercises in their manuscript pad. Their eagerness to get at the colouring pencils to colour code the notes makes them forget their embarrassment (if indeed they ever felt any) and so the situation dissipates - in every sense of the word.

There are other fragrance issues which cause me less embarrassing, but more serious problems. I have a great sensitivity to fragrance and strong smells give me an instant migraine. I have to avoid certain washing-up liquids for this reason. It's a shame and I'd love to help with the dishes, but there it is. Sorry! Some of the adult gents feel inclined to slosh about generous portions of Old Spice before they come to their lesson. Lynx is the worst and I'm reaching into the medicine cabinet the second I've said, 'Good bye'. Ladies' perfume is also a problem and not always in its relationship to my aching head. I'm not sure about Mrs Simpkins (the one married to the piles) - either she wears perfume which is some years out of date and has gone "off" or she "drinks a bit." With her eccentric personality it's difficult to tell, but she does carry with her the vague scent of stale, sweet alcohol. In many respects it doesn't matter either way - let the lady rock! My only concern is that she arrives at my door each week in control of a rather large Mercedes.

Gratefully yours, x

Dear Reader,

You must excuse me. I meant to introduce you properly to some of my pupils but, before I could recover from the tangent I'd gone off on, there was a knock at the music room door.

I imagine that you'll get to know quite a few of my pupils as the flow of absenteeism allows me to tell you. However, I don't think you'll ever get to know Mrs Simpkins. She has a will-o'the-wisp personality that's quite impossible to pin down. I know all about Mr Simpkins, but such knowledge is too graphic and hardly relevant to these letters. I'd hate to convey to you, dear reader, the burden of knowledge that I have in this area. All that I can tell you, in good conscience, is that I suspect she has a secret penchant for dry sherry and a tendency to insist upon playing music about four grades too difficult for her. Her performance isn't improved by the fact that she has a clinical inability to play more than two consecutive notes in a steady, consistent tempo. The final nail in the coffin of hope for anything like a musical performance is driven home when I bear testimony to her unique method of manicure. She possesses talons of preposterous proportions, each of which taper into a nicotine stained, downwards curved point. I have to admit that I worry for her safety and I begin each week's lesson with horrific premonitions of her leaving with her fingers bleeding while I'm left to pick out fragments of bony debris from between the keys of my piano. So far we've lived to tell the tale, but I'm not complacent and I remain vigilant at all times.

Maybe it's the precarious addition of dry sherry that really gives me cause for concern because other pupils with manicure issues don't keep me awake at night. Anabelle, a young lady in her late teens, sports extreme nail extensions. Instead of tapering into curls the tips lie straight and true ending in a harsh, flat edge. I did once suggest that she needed to trim these extremities for the sake of her piano technique. Her dominant sense of fashion and grooming was highly offended by the suggestion and I didn't dare venture the topic again. I didn't think she was emotionally strong enough to entertain the thought a second time. Mercifully, when her exam date was looming, her hands took on a more human form for a brief period of time.

I've already introduced young Gregory to you, or at least I've introduced you to his internal gastronomic combustion system. I'll grant you that this hardly describes the lad, but it expresses him perfectly. I suspect that Gregory was something of a surprise to his parents, born to them very late on in their married life. I get the idea that they've remained surprised ever since. There's no doubt that they dote on their darling but they convey the impression that they've raised him at arm's length and held him by the tips of their fingers while they remain quite unsure of what to do with him. He's a bundle of physical and emotional complexities that are like a taut elastic band which could pling off in any direction without a second of warning. Nevertheless, he's an endearing chap that I can't help but like. He's a man of few words, but when he does speak his accent is a throwback from the Potteries during the time of the Industrial Revolution. When asked to play something he'll peer at me dispassionately through his thick spectacle lenses and say,

'It's reet tricky, thaht. Ah conner pleey it 'owt like thaht.'

In terms of lesson content it's difficult to know where to begin. Each half hour is a "by the seat of your pants" affair as there's no knowing what will occur. Because his eyesight is so poor I scan and enlarge any music I intend to attempt, but even when he can *see* the music it's hit and miss if he'll be able to *read* it. At times he can make good progress, but that's only when the moon and Jupiter are in alignment, and if the wind is in the right direction. (I really wish that I hadn't just chosen that analogy. This is Gregory I'm talking about!) Generally speaking, the traditional classical approach isn't the way forward for Gregory. In many ways it's quite a pleasant time as the pressure of achievement really isn't an issue here. Nobody is pushing for him to attain musical brilliance and his parents are just happy for him to have a good time and knock himself out on somebody else's piano for thirty minutes. I just have to hope that creative inspiration will meet me in the music room each week and see what transpires. The key to getting through the lesson is to keep ringing the changes. We'll spend a few minutes at the piano experimenting with combinations of dynamics, pitch and rhythm, then we'll move to the desk to trace over some treble clefs and colour code some note names before hopping back to the piano to try out some note groupings and attempt some listen and response exercises. At the

end of thirty minutes Gregory returns to his confused
parents in a state of euphoria (usually) and I retire to
a darkened room.

Gratefully yours, x

Dear Reader,

It's an endemic part of human nature to want to conform, to fit in and be seen to belong. I know that it's common for us all to assert our uniqueness and individuality, but at the end of the day we inevitably succumb to some sort of uniform. Bikers join groups and adopt the badge and regalia. Cyclists kit themselves out in the lycra paraphernalia - even if they're only cycling half a mile downhill. I remember the scientists at University decorating their lab coats with paintings and embroideries of their chosen field of study. A huge, muscle-bound bloke who wore a lab coat painted over with purple butterflies was a particularly memorable example of conforming to the current vogue.

Musicians are no exception. I have a horror of what I term the "Treble Clef Brigade." Some of the most sensible and mature pupils are often the most susceptible. After only one or two lessons the signs begin to show: their solitary music book will begin to be transported to lessons in a velcro fastened carry-case of alarming primary colours, emblazoned with treble clefs and inaccurately drawn crotchets and quavers. The ladies will adopt an unusual fashion sense and wear musical earrings large enough to give you a black eye and innumerable floaty scarves with notation (again inaccurately drawn) scattered amid a floral background.

I've developed an inverted scale of psychoanalysis based upon the number of music related accessories adopted. This hypothesis has been tested over a lengthy trial period and with a wide range of unbiased (i.e. ignorant) subjects. At choir it is my theory that the newest and most inexperienced members carry their music (which they can't yet properly read) in the most highly musically decorated cases. As such I feel it necessary to take my own music in a supermarket carrier bag. If I'm honest it's because I never feel that I've earned the right to use treble clef regalia until I've proved my worth and ability sufficiently. I'm not sure of the degree of professionalism required until I've earned my stripes.

Of course I'm making sweeping generalisations but I'm convinced that the theory is sound. The best example I ever heard of was a bass player who had a treble clef tattooed on his forearm. Just think about that for a moment - he's a bass player... No doubt he'll live to regret that tattoo! I guess it's a phase we all go through and once the novelty has worn off the balance will settle to normal proportions. Nevertheless, I advise you to wait a while before you choose a musical tattoo.

I'd like to pretend that I'm impervious to the lure but it can't be denied that I've conformed to club mentality. However, instead of wearing the regalia myself I've directed the addiction towards household furniture. I have an incurable inclination to rip up old music scores and use them to "up-cycle" and "distress" old furniture. In my defence I don't only use music but I rip up old dictionaries as well. Tacky MDF bookcases and CD towers have all been subjected to the same treatment to render them "shabby chic" and are now adorned with, marked copies of Handel's "Messiah". Annotations such as

"Breath now," "Boys only" and "SIT," show directions from bygone performances on the shelving.

Whether it's bumper stickers, denim waistcoats and rucksacks covered with badges or musical accessories, it's something that we all dabble in at one time or another. My heart bleeds when I see a young school girl with musical hair clips and I feel for her innate insecurity. I just nod my head wisely and keep my mouth shut - she'll grow out of it.

Gratefully yours, x

Dear Reader,

September is a precarious month for all teachers. After the children have enjoyed the relative warmth of the Summer holidays the weather begins to change as they start back to school and are herded back into the classrooms. The heating systems go on at about this time, ready to help the bacteria to incubate successfully. After the children have undergone a sufficient period of contagion they then come for their piano lesson. This provides optimum conditions for the transferral of the (by now) robust and healthy bacteria as we're locked in an enclosed space and forced to sit in close proximity to each other for the next twenty minutes. This should give sufficient time for a successful relocation of the micro-organisms. Over the course of the first couple of weeks one of them is bound to hit the mark.

It's a policy of mine to always house a box of tissues next to the piano, but it's rare that anybody is inclined to use them. It's only after earnest prompting that a token one is taken. I introduced Matthew to you some time ago and he is a prime example of this. How far should I let things go before I intervene? I suppose that, at the end of the day, it's his prerogative to coat the length of his sleeve. However, I do draw the line when he begins to smear his hands and fingers which will next be making contact with my very own piano keyboard. Surely it's better to try and deal with matters at the thin end of the wedge.

'Would you like a tissue? I think you're defrosting after coming in from the cold.' I begin.

Matthew merely shakes his head and continues playing.

'Perhaps you'd better take a tissue.'

Another shake of the head, followed by a sniff and more bars stumble by. The ubiquitous tongue, projected in concentration mode, is dealing with the situation at present. The jumper sleeve then joins in to help out a little. Nevertheless, the stream is continuous and we're soon back to square one.

'I think you'd better stop playing and blow your nose, maybe?'

'It's OK.' he replies and applies the sleeve once again. This time he overshoots his aim and begins to return to the keyboard with glistening hands and fingers.

'Stop playing now! Go and wash your hands and give your nose a good blow.'

Unabashed he shuffles from the piano to the downstairs "powder room." Some minutes later he returns significantly drier and showing no signs of embarrassment.

Although the situation hits critical mass at the beginning of the academic year, to a degree the situation is a permanent state of being throughout the whole of the calendar. Even the Spring and Summer months aren't tissue free. The culprit in most cases here is hay fever, which means that we're also dealing with runny eyes as well as a runny nose.

My friend, Mae, has been known to keep a stock of anti-bacterial wipes next to her piano and gives her piano keys a wipe down at regular intervals throughout the evening, finishing with a thorough cleaning session at the end of the night. We may well mock such a rigorous attitude but she had a very bad experience. I think it has scarred her emotionally and I believe it's at the root of her germ phobia. When I recall her ordeal I realise that runny noses are the least of my worries.

They say that a problem shared is a problem halved, but in this instance I could be of no help whatsoever. I called on Mae, ready to go out for the evening and as we walked into her music room she asked,

'Does my music room smell?'

'No.' I replied. 'What have you done?'

She sank onto the piano stool and, with her head in her hands, recounted the events of her traumatic evening. Fortunately the gruesome event took place during the last lesson of the the evening. A small girl sat at the piano with no hint that anything was amiss. Halfway through the lesson the child turned to Mae and just said four words.

'I don't feel well.'

Instead of keeping her head turned away from the piano she looked back at the music. Making no effort whatsoever to move away the child was then violently sick over the piano keyboard. Mae was then forced to spend the rest of the evening cleaning up (or cleaning *out*) her piano. She even had to remove all the wooden keys off the keyboard as the unpleasant substance had oozed between the notes. She'd done a sterling job with the disinfectant and by the time I arrived there was no hint of the earlier trauma. However, she told me that the smell lingered in her nostrils for days!

Gratefully yours, x

Dear Reader,

It's a foregone conclusion that, as a teacher, I spend an awful amount of time talking. There are those who might say that, for a woman, this shouldn't be a problem. It's not as natural as it seems, dear reader. All teachers suffer from this to varying degrees but the strain on an instrumental teacher's voice is constant. At no point during the day or evening can I say,

'Off you go to work on this by yourselves for ten minutes.'

Whilst I'm sure that in a classroom setting this may still be punctuated by questions and interruptions, it isn't necessarily constant. In fairness, it's also true that I never have to strain my voice by shouting. Instead, every few seconds I have to speak a word or two and there is a regular workout routine that my vocal cords have to contend with during every single lesson.

I usually begin, as I open the door, with,

'Hello. Have you had a good week? Have you done anything exciting?'

I say this every blasted lesson! I keep intending to open the door and say something original but the dye is cast and the usual banalities leap out of my mouth before my brain has kicked into gear. I then initiate the lesson by suggesting a few scales. As the pupils begin to try to find their fingers I'll take a sip of water, or more likely a gulp of cold tea. It's at this point that things could get dicey. Very often random words tumble out of my mouth for no apparent reason and I have to do some swift thinking to turn my recent statement into something more coherent. When a student is playing scales of more than one octave the technique is to use your fingers in a specific order. You must tuck your thumb under after finger three, then again after finger four, and again after finger three - until you get to the top. Finger four is always a weak finger and a certain amount of dexterity is necessary for the manoeuvre. It's commonplace for a student to try and avoid using this finger and only tuck after finger three - which means you'll run out of fingers before the end of the scale. During scales practice I find it necessary, between sips of tea (definitely now very cold) to exclaim in firm tones,

'Four, tuck.'

I can't tell you how hard I have to concentrate to prevent any unfortunate spoonerism from occurring.

This reminds me of a lesson I had with Mae when I was about Eighteen, when we were working on my grade eight pieces. I was pegging my way through Mozart's Sonata in F major (K332) and my right hand thumb had developed a certain fascination for the note F and kept holding it down when it should have been released. Despite several gentle reminders from Mae my thumb persisted in keeping in contact with the aforementioned note. As a last resort she found it necessary to mark my copy and above the bar in question wrote, "F off!" I was easily shocked back then and blushed profusely before we both fell about laughing.

Once I'm safely over the hurdle of prompting fingering in scales it's time for us to work on the current piece of music that the pupil has been practising. (Bless my naïve optimism.) Every bar or so it's necessary to prompt the player in relation to certain aspects of the music. For example,

'B flat, remember.' - next bar - 'Rest in the left hand, let go of the note.' ("F off" springs to mind). 'Steady tempo, don't rush just because you see quavers.' (Silly me in presuming that there is such logic behind the hasty rendition of the notes.) 'Hands together.' (I have to fight off the urge to add, 'Eyes closed' to the remark. I certainly feel the need to pray.) And so it continues. More sips of water (or cold tea) are now required.

When I'm conducting a lesson I make notes of what we've covered that day and what the pupil needs to practice, so that parents are aware of the work we've done and can make sure they're working on the right material at home. (My persistent optimism is astounding, isn't it?) It often happens that I can be writing one thing whilst attempting to finish saying something entirely different. This provides ample opportunity for more incomprehensible garbage to escape through my teeth making my vocal cords work hard to no good effect. Either that or the notes in the lesson diary become utter nonsense. It takes some swift thinking to recover the situation and sometimes it's plain impossible. The only course open to me then is to admit that I've written a load of rubbish and explain that I'll have to start writing again, once again preying on the good nature of my overworked larynx.

After more sips of cold tea (I've given up all pretence of drinking healthful water now) I explain what needs to be practiced during the week and bid the student farewell. After all that cold tea nature calls, so please excuse me before my next pupil arrives.

Gratefully yours, x

Dear Reader,

We piano teachers can be a funny bunch. I suppose that's true of all people groups but I'm especially conscious that it's an easy assumption to make when thinking about music tutors. Maybe it's because we spent a large portion of our childhood and teenage years rattling up and down scales for hours, and slogging note by note through impossible Bach Fugues. The exam syllabus has changed considerably over the years (I'm not going to make even the vaguest reference to the academic downgrade here at all!) When I first met my husband I was practising for my grade 8 piano exam which was an integral part of the Oxford A Level syllabus. The list of scales included over two hundred permutations, which took a good two or three hours to work through if I intended to practise the whole set in one go. Just one of the three set pieces was a Sonata which was over twelve pages long and, because you weren't allowed any photocopies, I had to turn my own pages in the exam. This meant that I had to memorise chunks of music and turn when a hand was free. On top of that I had to memorise specific extracts of music from a seven hundred page opera for the written A Level exam. We had an exciting courtship, as you can imagine.

I know of a bygone piano tutor who adopted an "open house" policy for his pupils each Sunday and would give afternoon tea whilst hosting a Scales Party. He must have laid on some mighty fine cakes to entice anybody to attend, let alone induce them to join in. I'm not sure I could handle so much excitement. I can just picture the scene:

A row of girls wearing their best Sunday pinafores with ribbons in their hair. There'd be just a token boy or two sitting sulkily up in the corner, fidgeting because their mother had tied their ties too tightly around their throats. (I feel a similar urge myself at times.) The earnest piano tutor would be overly hearty in his welcome and would break the ice by performing a few scales himself.

'I'll just get the party started and warm the piano up. I'll play a couple of scales to lead the way.' says the teacher.

A thunderous rendition of F sharp harmonic minor in contrary motion over two octaves followed by C minor in thirds with two hands over four octaves sets the bar high. He turns to his little audience with an overbearing grin to see who is next to take the limelight. The row of girls now look like so many frightened rabbits under the glare of looming headlights and the boys have skulked further into the shadows of the corner of the room. There can be no escape as their lift home isn't for another hour or so and there's not a chance their parents will be early in picking them up - they've a couple of hours to themselves on a Sunday afternoon. The children's only hope is to resort to tea and cake and try and look busy.

Maybe I'm wrong. Maybe they're all dead keen to show off their proficiency. Perhaps Lavinia shoots her hand into the air.

'And now Lavinia will play for us D major, two octaves with right hand only.' introduces the teacher.

(Polite applause ensues.)

A stumbling rendition bolsters the confidence of the onlookers and little Joey emerges from the corner, keen to prove his worth.

'Ah, Joey. Splendid!' encourages the teacher. 'Joey will play for us A major with two hands over two octaves.'

Take that Lavinia! Both hands, do you hear? My goodness, this could go on all night! I hope the teacher provided plenty of cakes to keep their energy levels up.

I can't imagine such a Sunday afternoon standing much chance of success with today's students and I for one am not man enough to broach the venture. It wouldn't work in our home anyway. I can't find the piano on a Sunday as it's likely to be buried under a pile of ironing. Such a mentality isn't as rare as you might hope and there is a bizarre tendency amongst piano teachers to cook up strange scenarios. Sometimes Mae and I will spend an evening in the pub reading through the letters page of a music tutor's periodical sharing various piano teacher's droplets of wisdom (a gripping read, as you can imagine). They say that truth is stranger than fiction and I can assure you that my imagination couldn't make this lot up. It certainly makes for entertaining reading and is an excellent accompaniment to a pint.

Building finger strength is one of the main issues for a beginner when starting to play the piano. The only real solution is regular practice of scales in addition to regularly working on pieces of music. Just like any physical exercise, finger muscles are developed gradually. I once read a bizarre account of a teacher who wrote in to a musicians' periodical to share her miraculous tip. She suggested that tutors follow her example in chopping up erasers into small slithers to wedge between the piano keys to create extra resistance and so build strength quicker. What was the editor thinking of in giving her column inches? Didn't Schumann try a similar short-cut by making a strap for his fourth finger? The damage done to his hand was so severe that it permanently wrecked his performance career. Although, if I remember correctly, the vote is still out on whether it was this or the latter stages of syphilis which caused the damage .

Either way, don't try this at home folks!

Gratefully yours, x

Dear Reader,

I know that I am extremely fortunate to be able to indulge in the luxury of teaching individuals on a one-to-one basis. It gives far more scope for quality learning and provides the best potential for good progress. Because this style of teaching is, by necessity, the most expensive it is most often conducted on a private basis. Only in one school have I ever known this type of lesson to be completely free to the pupil. You'd think that, in consequence, I'd only get rich pupils coming for lessons and I'm sure that in many areas this would be the case, but that's not been my experience. Instead, I've found that my students tend to be from families that are willing to sacrifice and go without so as to provide their children with the opportunity to learn to play. Having to pay for lessons automatically provides a filter which sieves off those who can't really be bothered - they soon want to stop wasting their own time and money. No matter how exasperated I might think I feel, I know that the situation is infinitely better than any other setting. I've taught in classrooms and I've taught in groups - and I'm glad of the experience, if only to serve as a reminder for comparison.

During my A Level studies I took on a night class teaching keyboard techniques to a group of OAP beginners. It makes my palms sweat just to think of that time. The vast majority of the group were complete beginners and just a couple were technically advanced - if only in their own opinion. The whole concept was unworkable from every point of view, but I had my bread to earn and a term to fill. Even if I say so myself, I did a good job of arranging short pieces of music into basic chord shapes for the beginners, simple melody lines for the slightly more knowledgeable and a combination of left and right hand material for the more advanced. The idea was that, after initial explanation and demonstration, they could each practise their own part with headphones on as I walked around the room and helped out where needed. After a while the plan was to overlay all the parts and make a keyboard "orchestra." Whilst the principle was (and is) feasible it was actually the stuff of nightmares. I hadn't thought to reckon with a general inability to count up to four and I didn't factor into the equation the overbearing personality of certain individuals.

I know from personal experience that counting to four isn't as easy as it might at first seem. When the person on your left has to fit in eight quavers and the person on your right needs to play two minims to your steadily held four beat semibreve it can be nigh-on impossible to stay put. Instead there is an uncontrollable urge to rush in and join the crowd. Even after rearranging the keyboards into groups (safety in numbers) a steady tempo of four was out of their reach. Generally speaking they were just so thrilled at the joy of their own performance that they were deaf to the other players. Actually, that's not quite accurate - if only they were deaf to the other players and had stuck to their own music. What they were deaf to were my entreaties and directions. Why on earth was I standing at the front and waving my arms about? Nobody was watching!

Over time progress did take place and in some small measure there was a glimmer of hope for success. The effect wouldn't have been too displeasing if the overall sound wasn't drowned out by one particular performer, an old man named Gerald. Gerald became a constant companion to my thoughts. He had a certain amount of technical skill but he had far too bloated an opinion of himself and his abilities. I rather think that he was expecting to change places with me at short notice. He was unfortunately hampered by the fact that he had an irregular sense of timing and was seemingly hard of hearing - either he was partially deaf or he was totally ignorant, it was difficult to tell which. Unfortunately there was a single, decrepit electric organ in the room and Gerald took possession of this at the first instance and refused to relinquish ownership ever afterwards. Not only was there a volume control next to the lower keyboard manual but there was a volume pedal at the right hand side of the pedal board. Sensitive management of either of these mechanisms would have solved all of my problems. However, a war was at work over the volume slider next to the keyboard. I'd set the volume to an acceptable level before the lesson began but it was soon moved (by Gerald) to the limit of its scale. Over the course of the evening the slider would go up and down like a yo-yo. I even tried wedging some blu-tac in the recess of the lever, but to no avail. Gerald insisted on commandeering control and could only be content when the volume was up to full capacity.

This in itself would have been bad enough, but it wasn't the sum total of the trouble that Gerald caused. Despite repeated attempts to explain that the pedal operated by the right foot was a volume control the message somehow never got through and he persisted in a technique similar to that of a wind operated harmonium. Gerald's right foot pumped up and down in a rhythm steadier than any of his melody lines ever displayed. The result was a bizarre blaring and receding of noise as his foot moved up and down. During the course of the evening the volume level gradually rose and fell every second or so, from being almost imperceptible to becoming eye-wateringly loud. The effect made you feel quite sea sick. It's no wonder that the other players in the group struggled to maintain their own part. Gerald was utterly oblivious (or utterly unconcerned) with the devastation that was wrought behind his back and was impervious to any demands contrary to his own wishes. By the end of that term I believe that the pharmaceutical counter in a nearby branch of Boots had experienced such a rise in profits, from an unexpected increase in sales of headache medication, that it had enabled several successive managers to retire on a fat pension and leave the rat race forever.

No matter how bad I think a student might be doing I only need to remember my adult evening class and all doubts are laid to rest. Top quality music education is underway and everything is fine and dandy!

Gratefully yours, x

Dear Reader,

I think that perhaps the only drawback to playing the piano is that it can, at times, make for quite a lonely existence. Every instrumentalist has to spend long hours practising alone but most other instrument groups eventually get together for some sort of performance. For string, woodwind and brass players there are all sorts of orchestras, wind bands and brass bands to join in with. Pianists can join in with orchestras and quartets, but only if they have reached an exceptionally high standard. There is always the possibility of playing duets in a cosy twosome, if you're lucky enough to have a friend of about the same standard of ability. Other than that - you're on your own. In fact, that's the very point of the piano. You can be your own soloist and at the same time provide your own accompaniment. Thankfully, I also play flute and so I have had the best of both worlds. You just can't beat playing in an orchestra or a wind band. I still harbour the ambition to learn to play the soprano saxophone and play in a swing band. The fingering is very similar to flute fingering, so maybe I'll give it a go one day.

At school I was one of those awkward children that never managed to fit in. I hated pop music and when asked if I was going to the school disco I could only look confused because I simply couldn't understand the question. Were they joking? Did anybody ever really go to these things? I just couldn't comprehend it. It wasn't until I started to play the flute and got to a standard where I could join the school orchestra that I finally found a world in which

I belonged. I wasn't one of the best, but it was a world that I could understand.

My life reached something of a pinnacle when I made it to the prestigious position of first flute in the school orchestra, just in time for a concert. We were playing Haydn's "Surprise Symphony" and at that time I had something of a crush on the percussionist. I was especially excited for the concert as the first flutes sat at the edge of the stage, right next to the timpani (and therefore the timpani player). If you know the symphony at all you'll know that there are many little musical jokes throughout the piece, the most famous of all is a sudden loud chord at the end of an otherwise quiet theme. The jolting "crash" is provided by the timps, which is why the Germans often refer to the piece as the symphony "mit dem Paukenslag," (with the kettledrum stroke). It's easy to see that percussion plays an important role in the piece.

The seating around the music stands was a little cramped (school orchestras probably being better attended all those years ago) and, as we sat waiting for the lights to go up, I whispered to my fellow first flautist to ask if she could see the music well enough. Would she like me to shove over a bit? Keen to be accommodating to my colleague's comfort I gently shuffled my seat a little to the right. Just as the lights went up and as the conductor lifted the baton I fell off the edge of the staging (still perfectly seated on my chair) headlong into the timps and into the arms of the handsome percussionist. Well, they weren't expecting that, were they?

Don't ask me how, but apparently not many people noticed outside of the orchestra. Maybe it was a combination of a trick of the changing lights and the sound of the audience's anticipatory applause, as the conductor walked to take her place in front of the orchestra, but I managed to re-establish myself on the stage without overall detection. I picked up a bar or two late and the show went on. I think that scuppered any hope of a chance I had with the handsome percussionist though. Perhaps it was also at that point that I decided to concentrate on piano studies. It appears that Haydn has a lot to answer for in the direction that my life has taken.

Gratefully yours, x

Dear Reader,

When I refer to my period of residency in the Broom Cupboard I'm not necessarily always referring to the same one. I've had periods of occupation in various "cupboards" of a generic type over the years. My current place of address is one of the nicest, now that Spring is on the horizon and I've finally figured out how to turn the radiator off. It's relatively spacious and it's clean and tidy. The one enduring feature of all of these habitats is that they are *safe*. I don't mean that I'm securely hidden from an imaginary source of malice. I mean quite literally what I say - they are physically safe.

"How can teaching the piano ever allow me to be in physical danger?" I hear you ask, dear reader. I will tell you, and it's no laughing matter. Some years ago I was working with a local primary school and was asked to help out at their Harvest Festival service held in the nearby church. If I could just play a couple of hymns and accompany the children in a little song it would be greatly appreciated. Where was the harm in that? I knew the hymns well enough and I'd played "Cauliflowers Fluffy, Cabbages Green" plenty of times with my own children. Even now I can hear the bass line in my head, "Ba ba ba dum, da dum, da dum dee do - ahh." Catchy!

The day of the service arrived with no sense of impending doom. I arrived early to see what sort of instrument I'd be playing and to give me time to be calmly organised. I need to mention here that pianists have significant commitment issues. They are quite incapable of remaining faithful to the same instrument. String players, brass players and woodwind players can take their own instrument with them to their lessons, exams and performances. Sadly, not so with the pianist. There's no knowing what we'll pair up with from one day to the next. It's a sad fact of life and it's something that you learn to expect. Actually, there are slight deviations in the brass sector where they sometimes can't be bothered to lump their own instrument around and if there's the chance of a loan they just take their own mouthpiece for the sake of hygiene. Mix-ups happen too, of course. When my daughter was taking her grade five flute I assured her that I'd got it all sorted and bid her jump into the car. When we arrived at the exam centre I found, to my horror, that I'd not picked up her flute but had got mine instead. It's difficult to explain how playing a different instrument is so tricky. You blow in the same place and the keys are in the same place - but it feels totally alien. The tone and response is so very different from instrument to instrument. She did very well, under the circumstances, but I think I cost her a distinction that day.

Upon entering the church, ready for the school Harvest service, a frail old lady welcomed me and offered to escort me to the organ. OK, so there wasn't a piano. I guessed that I could manage, although "Cauliflowers Fluffy" would sound a trifle bizarre with reed and diapason stops. I also worried a little that being sat away from the children could create timing issues. If the organ pipes are high up there can be a significant time delay in the sound reaching the congregation in the lower levels. (It sounds like an extract from Dante's "Inferno.") The old dear led me to a narrow, winding stone staircase. I became genuinely concerned for her safety (not my own, as yet) as she began to climb the steps. For some portion of the climb there was a sheer drop to the left of the staircase until the wall of the upper balcony took the place of a bannister. I wondered if I should offer to help her but she steadily wound on in rotating steps until we reached the balcony where the organ was situated. I don't mind admitting that I'm not comfortable with heights but I saw no concern for real alarm. As we came into the open space I scanned the area and found the organ backing onto the edge of the balcony. I sat at the stool and tried to gather my wits. Inches behind me was a sheer drop. There was no safety rail, only a low wall about thigh high. Once I was seated on the tall stool there was nothing between me and a free sky diving experience. By this point I was definitely out of my comfort zone, but I can't say that I was positively afraid - yet.

The stalwart warden began to descend to the lower regions, but I didn't worry about her now, she would have to fend for herself. I was far too preoccupied with my own troubles. I'd turned the organ on and and my doom was set. It was unlikely that I'd live to tell the tale. As the machine powered up it began to shake violently. The pipe mechanism vibrated alarmingly as ancient systems attempted to summon up air to filter through the various pipes. The stool that my unfortunate behind was destined to be sat upon was an integral part of the pedal board. The wooden legs were securely attached to the framework of the lower pedal system and it shook in perfect union with the rest of the device. The only thing keeping the music on the stand were two metal pins designed for the purpose and the only thing keeping me seated at the organ was a paralytic inability to move.

I have very little memory of how the music was received. I think that I've repressed the memory as it's too traumatic to remain in my conscious thought. Bar by bar the hymns passed by. Any timing issues with the choir were probably excused on the basis of the immaturity of the singers - no doubt it added to the appeal. The worst times were the periods of inactivity, when all I could do was concentrate on the main task in hand - holding on for dear life.

At the end of the service I was again met by the ancient church warden. She seemed pleased with the morning's work and all had gone swimmingly as far as she was concerned. I tentatively made reference to the fact that I wasn't comfortable with heights and she seemed to perceive my shattered nerves. And so it was that the old dear packed away my music, took my arm and helped me down the stairs - very carefully and slowly.

Gratefully yours, x

Dear Reader,

What do you do when it's early in the morning, you're cocooned in a warm room and a persistent drone is repeating in the background? The answer is simple - you fall asleep. The only hitch in the proceedings is the unfortunate fact that you're supposed to be conducting a piano lesson. I'm not naturally a morning person and I can't for the life of me figure out why anybody would schedule their lesson for eight o' clock in the morning. I'm staggered to learn that I have pupils who do their piano practise at six o' clock before breakfast and school. There's no doubt that such application is evident in their playing ability, but it goes above and beyond the call of duty to my mind. Some years ago a friend studying Piano at a Conservatoire used to get up at five o' clock to practise because it was the only time she could be sure of booking a practice room for any useful length of time. Digital pianos have mostly done away with the necessity for such extreme measures in these enlightened days. Most students that I know of hack into their student finance at the start of term to buy a digital piano for their room and then live on pasta and beans until the next cheque comes in. There's always the odd phantom student roaming the corridors of the practice rooms during the early hours of the morning, but I can't be sure that they aren't a figment of the imagination or the result of some undigested cheese from the night before.

Alternatively, it's not unusual for me to be found seated at the piano in the small hours of the morning (not having yet got to bed) which might go some way to explain my drowsiness during the early school piano lesson rota. Thankfully I can boast that I have never actually fallen asleep during a lesson. It's been a close call at times but I have, as yet, escaped that ultimate shame. On innumerable occasions I have had to suggest that it might be beneficial to attempt a particular finger exercise again, being careful not to mention whose benefit the repetition is for.

I know of one teacher who was sharply awoken by the nodding jolt of her own head as she slipped into slumbering unconsciousness for just a second. The next couple of lessons were then spent in a cold sweat as she gripped her chair, with whitening knuckles should she "drop-off" again and slip off her seat as a result. Worse still is the case of the guitar teacher who fell totally asleep during a lesson. It's the stuff of nightmares! Imagine being awoken (as occurred in this instance) by the pupil's stark question,

'Am I boring you?'

Any possible answer forbids comment as the reply is as plain as the nose on your face!

Gratefully yours, x

Dear Reader,

When not ensconced in a broom cupboard on location I teach most evenings at home. When my children were very young I'd only teach for a few hours each week from home and the broom cupboard stage of my career was suspended for a considerable period of time. These few hours teaching meant that the kids' whole evening was dedicated "dad time" with whatever madness that inferred. It usually meant that they went to Nan's for a slap-up dinner and more choice of dessert than they had fingers. If they didn't dine out my husband would make camp upstairs and would read to the children all evening. This wasn't a pastime that was reserved for these evening only, it was something that we did all of the time. David used to read to me when I was pregnant, and as soon as the children could listen to Mr Men stories he'd read to them, at any time of the day. As the children grew older we'd all sit and listen together and the level of complexity of the stories grew along with the children. This tradition continued well into their teenage years. It got a bit tricky as the books became more mature and you could see David looking ahead, figuring out which swear words might need to be replaced. In the end we found that the kids were guessing more elaborate versions than those in print and so he just read what was in front of him. Sometimes we all got so gripped with the story line that he was coerced into taking days of holiday from his business to finish reading the book. We'd sit listening and eating chocolate and drinking tea whereas David was reduced to drinking squash to keep his vocal cords lubricated.

There are benefits to working from home but there are also distinct disadvantages. These points are very decided and not everybody can take to it. It's advantageous in that, if I have a cancellation, I can quickly pop a load of washing through the washer, or I can finish a few dishes. More often than not I'll put the kettle on and call David from his studio in the loft to join me with a brew for half an hour. Our relationship began around the vending machines at college and the ritual is now set in stone. There is also the luxury of not having to commute further than the staircase and traffic is never an issue - though the queue for the bathroom never seems to go down. However, this also means that I have to keep the house relatively neat and tidy for pupils and waiting parents. Not every music tutor finds this last prerequisite necessary, in fact there seems to be an unwritten code of honour where a direct relationship between clutter and apparent musicality is assumed. It seems that teaching music amid a confusion of untidiness marks you out as being especially creative - I'm obviously not that arty! An alternative is to keep only the room which houses the piano habitable and have parents waiting outside during lesson time. I'd feel particularly inhospitable if I acted in such a manner and so I make sure that the lounge is also presentable so as to act as a waiting room. My family will also offer to make you a brew if they're around and available.

Such openness does make you vulnerable and at times I've felt that it might have knocked the professional edge off the service that I offer, but I've begun to see that this might not be such a bad thing. When a student begins taking music lessons it's a brave undertaking. In essence you're laying yourself open to looking a bit of a fool, or it can at least feel that way. I always stress that music lessons are specifically for making mistakes in (otherwise you wouldn't be needing the lessons) and music practice should sound messy as you chop the music into bits to try and re-try sections. I can see now that having the echoes of family life going on in the background naturalises the situation to a degree. I'd taught Timothy for about four years until the time came for him to leave to go away to University. On his last lesson he told me that he felt like he was part of the family and that he was leaving home twice over. I did feel a lump in my throat and a tear in my eye when he told me that.

However, there were times when story time with dad would get a little out of hand and the children were a shade too excitable. When David was reading the Quidditch scenes from the Harry Potter books we felt bound to apologise to our neighbour for the noise that we'd made. If I was teaching and such a ruckus was going on upstairs I'd interject during the lessons to explain that my husband wasn't roasting the kids alive but he was reading aloud to the children and it must be getting to a particularly gripping part in the story. No doubt there were times when he was giving the kids a roasting but I hoped that my general statement would cover the situation. Although I'd made the lounge available as a waiting room I began to notice that, at story time, the pupils and parents would prefer to linger in the hallway rather than sit and wait in comfort. I'd spent ages fretting that the ambience didn't provide a sophisticated teaching environment and never guessed that such behind-the-scenes distractions could ever be a bonus.

Sadly, not all of the background noises were conducive. What can you do when you hear through an open bathroom door,

'Daa-aad, I'm fi-iinii-iished!'?

There really are no words. There can be no doubt concerning what the statement was about as the call was soon followed by the flushing of a toilet.

Even now the children are grown up the situation isn't simple. If it's not the dog snoring loudly or whimpering to be let out of the music room (or let back in to the music room) it's the engine of motorbikes revving up and down the driveway. Even the hens create a distraction. They've obviously watched the animated movie "Chicken Run" innumerable times and have managed to either fly over a six foot fence or to dig under it. We do have a stone garden ornament of a cockerel named "Rocky" and I hold him responsible. During a recent flute lesson proceedings were interrupted by my husband gathering up our hens found wandering around the driveway next to the music room window and heading off into the main road. He decided to lift one up to peer through the window to demonstrate his hen catching ability. This type of behaviour is not conducive to a seamless flute performance.

Gratefully yours, x

Dear Reader,

There is always some form of associated paraphernalia that comes with any sort of interest group. Rubber wrist bands go a long way towards helping us broadcast our affinity with particular partialities, rather like a personal bumper sticker. Even so, we always manage to find bizarre ways of spending our money to publicise our partisanship. Some of the accoutrements carried around by musicians are necessary, such as cork grease or instrument cleaners, but it's amazing how we find ways to justify gathering all sorts of bits and bobs for imagined "coolness factor" more than purposes of base utility.

As a young teenager I felt quite the rebel when purchasing cigarette papers, ostensibly to dry off the flute key pads after long periods of playing. This was in fact doubly "cool" because it implied that I was a dedicated musician who practised for long hours and so needed to dry off the key pads at intervals during playing. It also left hanging the possibility that I might use the papers for their original purpose and actually smoke them! Out of my peers I can't think of a single individual who would have really dared to smoke, but ownership of these packets of papers left the whole question open - you would never really know. Of course, the dichotomy of being a serious wind player and the detrimental effects that smoking has on a player's lung capacity never entered our precious skulls.

The potentially more dangerous accessory popular among wind players is the miniature screwdriver. I'm not directly referring to the item as being dangerous to our actual person or our contemporaries - though with sufficient provocation who knows? During my school orchestra days the concept in carrying this hazardous device inside your instrument case was to create a public display of your adeptness at performing minor alterations and repairs to your instrument on the hoof. I suspect that this was almost entirely vain pretence. If there were as many fumbling attempts at DIY repairs as there were screwdrivers in cases the repercussions would have been evident in resultant trips to our friendly, local instrument repair workshop. He would be driving a much flashier car by now if even half of the supposed repairs were ventured. I know that I never dared to wield the thing despite having two or three rattling around next to my flute.

A perfect example of how a little learning is a dangerous thing is exquisitely demonstrated in the personage of Bert. Bert was in his late seventies and came to me for both flute and piano lessons. Many people attend lessons in their later years and I'm glad that they do. Sadly Bert was not a healthy specimen and playing an instrument took its toll on the dear chap. He'd assemble his flute and as he began to play some warm-up exercises he'd begin to puff and perspire away. At intervals he'd stop to have a sit down, explaining that he had a heart condition and needed to take things easy. It was during these frequent breaks that the real trouble would start. Out would come the miniature screwdriver set and before long I'd be crawling around on my hands and knees, scouring the carpet for the tiniest of screws that had sprung off in the most unpredictable directions. This occurred with alarming regularity. Despite my gentle pleas for him to leave well alone his enthusiasm for constant "tweaking" was unabated and when I suggested that, if there was a genuine problem, he'd perhaps be better taking his flute along to a specialist (though there was no "perhaps" about it). Bert was visibly offended and I didn't like to pursue the topic further. He just couldn't help himself. I think that many years ago (in a previous life) Bert had been an engineer of sorts. Now his health was poor, his nerves were shot and his hands shook like leaves on a tree in a gale - but he didn't let that stop him. I had to admire his tenacity, even if it was sadly misplaced. His ultimate solution to the scattering of screws was to solder everything into place. Now I realise that I'm no expert, but I'm far from convinced that this was a good idea and I've a vague inkling that a minuscule amount of manoeuvrability is necessary to the smooth action of the keys. The level of wear on the pads must surely dictate the occasional loosening or tightening of screws (performed by a knowledgeable expert.) If this weren't the case surely all of these fixtures and fittings would be properly secured in the first place. Even if I am mistaken in this assumption I feel quite certain that great blobs of common o' garden flux shouldn't be utilised. I'm a great believer in the "make do and mend" ethos but even I accept that there are limits.

At least Bert's piano lessons were a more sedentary form of music making - he was sitting down at least. Of course it was necessary for him to use my instrument, pianos not being particularly portable. I had a grand piano at the time and, on no grounds whatsoever, would I lift up the lid during this lesson time. In lessons with other students I'd sometimes find it helpful to lift the piano lid to show the working mechanisms of the piano and so that the student could see the dampener board and the sustain pedal in action. Bert would have to use his imagination! In an early lesson he once told me that he tuned his own piano and had adjusted the pedal action to make it easier to use. I needed no further warning but kept the lid firmly shut from then on. The unfortunate trade-off of a more relaxed lesson at the piano was that the entire lesson would have to be spent playing. Those intervals of rest that Bert needed during a flute lesson provided some welcome respite and even scouring the carpet for wayward screws helped to while away the minutes. Nevertheless, a seemingly never ending half hour at the piano was a small price to pay for the assurance that my own instrument would still be intact at the end of the lesson.

Gratefully yours, x

Dear Reader,

On a more serious note I probably need to mention that being a music tutor is something that I genuinely believe has great worth. Of course it's a "job" and it's a very pleasant job, but it's far more than that. It's a vocation that I honestly treasure. I realise that I sound like I'm sitting in front of an interview panel, in fact I've said those very words in just that setting - but that doesn't detract from the earnest sincerity of my making such a statement. Being outside the mainstream system of education means that I'm mercifully free from external constraints, I'm free to speak from the heart. It's a shame that the reason I have the opportunity to share these private thoughts with you is because somebody hasn't bothered to show up for their lesson to benefit from these droplets of wisdom. Such is life!

I suppose that the standard verbiage would be that playing an instrument enhances personal means of expression and communication. It also improves numeracy skills (although in my case I'm not sure that this has been the case - or goodness knows how bad I'd be without this extra dimension). There's no doubt that all such advantages are true. Research has shown quite conclusively that playing an instrument improves your IQ and fires up activity in all areas of your brain. Music brings all of this and so much more.

I've already confided in you, dear reader, that as a child I was shy and awkward. For almost the whole of my school life I struggled to find my place, both socially and intellectually. The worst times were at the start of High School but my doom was set from my first years in Primary School. I must have been a serious young thing. It's a wonder and a mercy that God paired me up with an extrovert on a motorbike for a husband. I spent the first term of High School in a state of severe shell shock. When a guy asked me to go on a date with him I was genuinely confused. Why was he asking me? Who was he? I hardly knew him - No! Why on earth would anyone want to go to the school disco anyway? I was never really convinced that anybody actually attended these things. How could you stand the noise? Some years later I decided that I'd better find out what all the fuss was about and ventured out to a Night Club. Within half an hour I was calling my dad, begging him to take me home. I felt like I was at an auction in a cattle market! I've since learned to go out and have a good time, but under the safe escort of my extrovert husband.

At the tender age of fourteen I found something of an identity, as well as a certain amount of ability, as I became engrossed in the study of ancient heroes such as J. S. Bach and Franz Schubert. In the hallowed days of GCE O level I had to learn extracts of Bach's "Toccata and Fugue in D minor" and Schubert's "Trout Quintet" from memory. I found that, after hard work, I could understand the form of a four part fugue. The words "subject," "countersubject," "inversion" and "truncation" began to make hazy sense. It was like being initiated into an elite group. There were only about five of us in the class and, although I wasn't one of the brightest, I was at least one of the few. I can appreciate that this syllabus didn't attract the hordes and was exceptionally discriminatory, but I do wonder if in an attempt to make the subject more inclusive we've now excluded those who would revel in such study. It's possible that the subject content has become so diluted that it's become null and void. (I did warn you that I wasn't bound by the constraints of external governing bodies. Here speaks a musical snob of the old school.)

I had the same opportunities and challenges in the physics laboratory and I don't count it as loss that I was unable to join in the elite there and I imagine that others might experience the same thrill of belonging on becoming a valued member of the netball or rugby team. Well, I say that I can imagine it - I'm sure that the situation does occur, but my imagination can't actually summon up any images here. I was "that kid" who never got picked for the team (any team) and that was just fine by me. Even if the addition meant that the team gained an extra player they'd rather do without that extra number if that extra was me. I wonder if in an attempt to be inclusive we've actually precluded those who would most benefit and clipped the wings of those who might really fly in their chosen field. I notice that Sports Days are now team based so that no single person ever really wins. Sports Day was the worst day imaginable as far as I was concerned, but I would never want to take away the opportunity for somebody else to show their worth. I came top often enough in the spelling tests. Sports Day was somebody else's turn. Taking this line of thinking a little further, I saw the most ironic thing in a school corridor: At the end of a long, otherwise empty corridor, was a solitary classroom with a closed door on which there was the label "Inclusion Room." Is it just me or does that seem a little on the fishy side? I think I've made my point.

For me, the really golden days began when I first started to play the flute and the piano. Once again I wasn't the best and I never made it into the higher echelons of those chosen few favourites (or so it seemed at the time). I had to practice hard and none of it came easily, I'm not sure that it ever really does. Paradoxically, although I was never in the group of elite favourites, out of those small few of us that studied music at school I'm the only one who has remained in the subject for their chosen profession. There's no doubt that it's a precarious industry. If you're looking for a regular income and regular working hours - forget it!

Looking back I realise that perhaps I didn't need to be quite the introvert that I was. Perhaps it can actually be "cool" to be able to play 'Teddy Bear's Picnic' in a pub in Amsterdam and get free Grolsch for your buddies. Even churning out a few bars of Mozart isn't anything to be shy about, if only I'd known it. There must have been some appealing qualities to lure my husband over the threshold of the college Art Department and into the forbidden territory of the Classical Music Department refectory. Meaningful relationship building is always at its best over a vending machine coffee.

Gratefully yours, x

Dear Reader,

I really dislike going to the hairdressers. I'm led to believe that this isn't the usual kind of statement made by a woman. I don't particularly dislike actually having my hair cut and styled, but I don't like the constant chatter and questions from a relative stranger who should be giving her undivided attention to the scissors she is wielding next to my ears. I also don't appreciate having to pay through the nose for enduring the noise and the stress that I have to undergo for a basic trim. My problem is solved now that I've got a wonderful arrangement with Linda, who is a pupil of mine and is fortuitously also a mobile hairdresser. We tend to operate a swap where I exchange lessons for a regular trim. I think I'd much prefer to live in a cashless economy akin to the barter system of old. So long as both parties are satisfied with the trade and the taxman still gets his dues then all is well. I don't suppose it's workable as a long term economy system but at least I get my hair cut without having to endure the third degree. I don't mind putting the kettle on and chatting to Linda as she brushes and chops. At least I know her and she knows me. Maybe if you went to the same salon for years and your hairdresser became your friend it would be quite a pleasant exchange. It's the whole "getting to know you" in a prescribed setting that I can't abide. You're suddenly confronted with the prospect of having to spend a good hour with somebody you've never met before and it's usual for people to want to fill that time with chit-chat. I'd be more than happy to spend that time in total silence but I gather that this isn't socially acceptable and so the usual conversation instigator is employed.

'What do you do for a living?' asks the enthusiastic stylist.

Initially my hackles rise as I dislike the fact that we are assessed by our mode of employment. It's not always an accurate indicator of who we are. When the children were young all of my time was spent in cleaning up various types of mess, and while I'd be the first to admit that this is of prime importance, it hardly explains who I am. Nevertheless I do realise that a job description can give a handle on the essence of who you are as a person. It's a beginning, but this is the crux of my problem.

'I'm a piano and woodwind tutor.' I reply.

This is usually greeted by a shrill ascending and descending glissando followed by knowing looks from the stylists. I honestly don't say this kind of thing for effect. I don't pretend to any moral high ground, it's just that I'm useless at anything else. I can guarantee that the next comment will be something along the lines of,

'My kid has a keyboard.'

By now I'm resigned to the conversation veering off out of my control, on a totally incorrect tangent and all of my purist sensibilities start to sound the alarm. I do not play the electronic keyboard, I do not play the electronic organ or "Roll out the Barrel" and the latest song by Adele is not in my repertoire. I guess I should be grateful now as an entirely separate conversation is going on above my head (in every sense of the word) and in reality I'm free to sit quietly and hope that as the stylists chat my ears remain intact. Unfortunately I find that I still can't relax. Instead I feel myself becoming more and more stressed at being totally misunderstood and misrepresented. Even so, this is the best case scenario. The topic can go two ways and there is a second route that the conversation can take. Instead of the shrill glissando there now follows a disapproving pause before tight-lipped clipping continues as the stylists launch into a diatribe of their various bad experiences with music teachers at school. Whilst I freely admit that we do seem to attract a few mutants I don't appreciate being automatically bracketed alongside these few unpleasant specimens, nor is this exclusively applicable to music teachers. I could argue that all PE teachers are cruel and have serious anger management issues. I don't feel inclined to perpetuate such rumours and I also know that it's usually the familiar story of the few spoiling it for the many.

I know that my friend, Mae, also has the same trouble when she needs a haircut. She recently went to a new salon, it being the only one that could find time to give her a trim before she went away on holiday. The stylist was chatting to her colleague, full of news about her son's new electric keyboard and in an attempt to be friendly the hairdresser turned off the dryer to ask,

'Are you musical?'

Rather than sit with wet hair and unleash the whole cavalcade Mae, in her wisdom, simply replied,

'No.'

After that she was free to sit relatively quietly, with the minimum of 'uhms' and 'ahs' at specified intervals whilst not getting bound up in unwanted interest in her mode of occupation.

I do get tired of being bound by stereotype and I've a short fuse once the "bandwagon" gets rolling on full momentum. Unfortunately, I did once misread a whole social situation at a friend's Fortieth birthday party. Upon joining the guests over drinks in the kitchen our host introduced me to his friend.

'Terry, this is Sharon. She's a piano teacher.'

At this point I usually die quietly inside and wait to see which route the conversation will follow - just as in the hairdressers. Terry is a massive body builder and a biker. Removing the pint from his lips he replied with the stock retort and, with a knowing twinkle in his eye, nodded sagely to his companions.

'I've always wanted to play the piano. It's something I'd really like to do. I wish I'd learned.'

I've spent my whole life having fun poked at my choice of pastime (or it can sometimes feel that way). All those years at High School came flooding back to me - the trendy, popular guys scoffing in sarcastic tones. Maybe my reaction was hormonal, a result of the mid-life crisis (it was a Fortieth birthday party after all) but something inside snapped. Instead of listening meekly until he'd finished with his clever derision, as innumerable times before, I calmly laid down my wine glass and made my comeback.

'It's not funny, you know. I've spent my whole life listening to comments from people like you. I can honestly tell you that I've just about had enough.

Tolerance is a one way street, I find, when you don't want to follow the crowd. Just tell me, what key is this song we're listening to in? You can't, can you? I could - if I was interested enough to try. Instead, because I prefer to play Mozart instead of Motorhead, you think that's cause for criticism. If you think you can play - come and find out, it's tougher than you think.'

Poor Terry looked genuinely upset and stammered,

'I'm so sorry. I didn't mean to offend you. I really do wish I could play - I've always regretted not being able to. I'm quite jealous of the fact that you're musical. I'd love to play Mozart but I've no idea where to even start!'

I could have died. I felt thoroughly ashamed of myself and my poor husband (standing next to me during the whole catastrophe) looked pretty ashamed of me too. I took a large gulp from the wine glass I'd relinquished and gave Terry a most heartfelt apology.

In this instance who was it who was prejudiced - basing assumptions of character on first impressions? Me! After profuse apologies and Terry's kind acceptance of my most sincere regret at my outburst we spent the evening chatting away like old friends and he has been my most long-standing pupil. He's become a good family friend and he has watched my family grow, week by week for more than a decade. I was wrong to assume that a muscle-bound biker wouldn't really be interested in the study of classical music.

If I take a step back and look at myself, as I am today rather than what I was as a school girl, I imagine that people could say the same about me. Mae and I regularly patronise the same pub and we are known and welcomed there. David and I once visited this same pub to have a meal after a long day riding on the motorbike. Nobody recognised me in my bike gear and we were treated to frosty stares as we found a vacant table. The only thing that was different about me, compared to previous visits, was my jacket and bike helmet. During the Summer holidays I often skid into an out-of-term lesson straight from a trip on the motorbike and if the pupil is a few minutes early they have to wait while I clamber out of leather bike gear before I can give my attention to Grieg or Schumann. There's no such thing as "normal" and it served me right! I'm just relieved that Terry was as forgiving as he was. It's more than I deserved.

Gratefully yours, x

Dear Reader,

Although the vast majority of my time is spent sitting on my bottom, pointing at music and doing very little else (save talking a lot) there are times when I do actually exercise my fingers on the keyboard myself and I do try to carve some time aside in which I can play for my own pleasure. I also play accompaniments for my woodwind pupils and in preparation tests for exams. Over many years I've also played at innumerable weddings and funerals.

It's rather humbling to acknowledge how alike most funerals are. Most of us grow up, go to school, fall in love, have a family, grow old and then die. There's a reassuring sameness about it all. I've always struggled to understand why the officiator at a funeral has to go through the whole rigmarole of giving a resumé of the deceased's life throughout the ceremony. Those of us who knew the deceased already know what's being said and those who didn't hardly care. It's the few sorrowful exceptions to the rule that stand out from all of the rest.

I played at the funeral of a young teenager who had tragically died in a foolish traffic accident. From all of the surrounding gossip it transpired that the possibility of an accident had been on the cards for some time and the wonder was that calamity hadn't happened sooner - not that this lessened the grief of the relatives. Even more sorrowful, as I thought, were the testimonies that friends and family gave during the service. The only thing that anyone could say was how much they'd enjoyed sitting watching TV together. Other than being as careful as you can on the roads there's no assurance that we'll avoid a traffic accident but I came away from that day determined to make the most of every day and not waste it behind a flickering screen.

Ordinarily I'm quite immune to the grief that surrounds me and I play through the hymns and various other pieces of music unaffected. However, there was one occasion that really did affect me and I really struggled to perform my duties as I blinked through the tears. A young man who was in one of the forces had committed suicide, leaving behind him a young wife and a small daughter - an acquaintance of my children who were the same age. Apparently some question of conduct had been raised and, although it was shown that he was clear of any tarnish, he'd said that he couldn't live with the cloud hanging over him. The church was filled to overflowing and the sense of shock and loss was palpable. To this day I don't know how I managed to keep playing on through the verses. I don't think many of the congregation could keep up with the singing despite my efforts.

Ours is quite a rural community although pasturage is gradually giving way to housing estates and, as dairy farming becomes more and more of a struggle, sectioned paddocks for horses are more common than grazing land for cattle now. Nevertheless, small farms still exist and for the most part the farmers form a friendly co-operative and pull along together. However, a long standing feud has existed between the Copes and the Hardacres. Nobody quite remembers the root of the trouble, it's probably buried with bygone generations. Frank

Cope had handed the bulk of the dairy farming down to his son some years past, but in his late eighties he still maintained a large poultry concern and also raised a number of porkers. Only a few weeks previously he was mucking out as normal, but now I was playing for his funeral. From all that I'd heard it was to be quite an affair. No expense had been spared - the family had even gone so far as to recruit a particular breed of Shire horse from quite some distance away to pull the hearse.

I normally aim to be seated at the organ before any of the congregation are likely to arrive so that I can make sure that I am comfortably established and my music is organised. I have a selection of appropriate music to play quietly in the background for when people begin to arrive. Music such as Bach's "Jesu Joy of Man's Desiring" is good, or a more modern favourite of mine is Lloyd Weber's "Pie Jesu" which I have arranged for organ from a four part choral piece that I have sung with the choir I belong to. I make sure that I've quite a few alternatives so that there are no awkward pauses until the funeral party arrives. It seemed that Frank Copes was going to be late - as he usually had been in his life. I was getting towards the bottom of the pile of my music and there was no sign of the funeral directors. I'd not got a watch on (I can't wear a watch as it makes my wrist and fingers ache) but I presumed that the hearse would be along soon. Bach's Prelude Number One was the last piece of music I'd got to go at and there was still no sign of the coffin. A little nifty thinking on the fly and a dominant seventh chord that Bach never intended gave me opportunity to go back to the beginning and play it all again. Although I do like the piece it is plausible to suggest that this music could easily be described as repetitive, and so further repeats which weren't part of the original composition were getting beyond mundane. I'd have to start from the top of my music pile again. Where could the funeral party have got to? I heard some muttering in the front pew and I caught the words,

'Even the organist has run out of music and started again. What's going on?'

They must have been one of the first to arrive, I was hoping that nobody would notice! I could see the church warden and tried to catch her eye. She shuffled over to reassure me that the hearse had arrived and that the funeral could begin soon - they were just waiting for the police to arrive. She said that she'd explain everything else later and with that enigmatic reassurance she left me to my ad lib repetitions until the coffin finally began it's journey down the aisle and the service was underway.

As the funeral progressed and the vicar recounted the usual life history my eyes wandered. Looking out of the windows, through the stained glass, I could just see the top of a policeman's helmet as he walked the circumference of the building. I was later told that the delay had been caused by a punch-up between the Copes and the Hardacres. The Hardacres had taken umbrage at either being invited, or not being invited to the service - it hardly matters which. After the horses had drawn the coffin away and were turning into the church driveway they'd blocked off the funeral car carrying the Cope family members and had hoisted the chauffeur out of the driver's seat. Steven Hardacre, a particularly feisty member of the clan, had then taken the keys out of the car's ignition and thrown them into a nearby field to cause further obstruction. Not being a family to take such treatment on the chin the Copes, regardless of their mourning finery, took instant revenge with their fists (no doubt the hope and intention of the Hardacres) and a hearty punch-up was going on as I was doing the rounds (quite literally) with J. S. Bach. The service was finally able to proceed once a police escort began circling the vicinity, ensuring that any scores remaining to be settled would wait until a more polite juncture.

Perhaps playing at weddings has a little less strain on the emotions though the call to play at such functions is diminishing. This may not only be due to the fact that perhaps less people are getting married but also because those that do wed prefer a CD of their favourite songs rather than live music. At our wedding Mae and her husband played an arrangement of Mozart's "Romance," the second movement of "Eine Kleine Nachtmusik," on flute and pipe organ during the signing of the register. I think that a CD lacks that special authenticity when compared to a live performance. Nevertheless, I realise that musicians aren't always that easily come by and I can also understand that the wedding couple might not want obscure music that they've never heard of on their special day.

Once I was playing at the wedding of a young couple and it was obvious that they would have no empathy for Grieg's "Morning Song" or Satie's

"Gymnopedie" - I was pretty sure they'd never have heard of them. Trying to think of more contemporary alternatives that would still carry the right ambience I suggested various Disney themes. We decided upon "Tale as Old as Time" which is a sublime melody and has won much acclaim. It has such a haunting melody line and was surprisingly effective on the gentler stops of the pipe organ - it was so moving it made your skin tingle. Only on the day of the wedding did I see my mistake. As I glanced at the printed Order of Service I saw, to my horror, that "Beauty and the Beast" would be signing the register!

Gratefully yours, x

Dear Reader,

I do wonder what often motivates people to want to learn to play. With adult learners the answer is obvious and that it's a genuine desire to play an instrument. With younger pupils the answer is less simple. There are, of course, parents who genuinely desire to give their children the opportunity to learn to play. The benefits that playing music offers and the sense of satisfaction that learning a musical instrument gives are reason enough, but I'm not convinced that this is always the underlying cause for bringing a child to lessons. In fact I'm of the opinion that this is more likely the exception rather than the rule. I think that to many students music lessons is just another "club."

Whilst I'm sure that it's a good thing to encourage our youngsters to have a healthy interest in a variety of topics the concept can be, and often is, taken to absolute extremes. I've known seven year old children submitted to a weekly schedule that would make me shake in my boots. On top of breakfast club each morning (which I still don't understand the need for) and then a day at school, each evening has it's own allocated activity (or in extreme cases even two clubs on certain evenings!) A typical timetable could look like this:

Monday: Swimming Lessons

Tuesday: Scouts

Wednesday: Football, followed by Piano Lesson

Thursday: Taekwondo

Friday: Dance Lessons (Ballet, Jazz and Tap)

Saturday: Drama Group (morning)

Sunday: Horse Riding (morning and afternoon)

Apart from wondering how on earth parents can afford all of this, when does the poor kid get chance to learn their spellings, read a book or simply relax and do some colouring-in? I suppose that the simple answer is - they don't! I've known reading and homework be squeezed in at the pool side whilst waiting for the earlier swimming class to finish. I suppose the bare essentials get fitted in somehow, but there's no time to just "be." Also, I'm not very knowledgeable in the science of anatomy, but I'm sure that Ballet uses very different muscles from Taekwondo - and too much of this mixture at a young age can't be beneficial. This does however explain why some pupils never do any music practice between lessons.

For quite a few years I made the honest mistake of thinking that I was being generous in giving pupils colouring-in to do as homework. I'd photocopy some of the illustrations in their tuition book so that they could colour over the black and white copy with pencil crayons and think I was giving them a treat instead of doing piano practice. I honestly thought I was giving the child an excuse to legitimately relax and play colouring instead of practising scales and pieces. It took a long time for it to sink in that many of these kids, despite owning a Nintendo DS or Kindle Fire, don't actually have any colouring crayons.

I used to spend hours upon hours lying on the floor, resting on my elbows with my heels kicking in the air as I coloured pictures resting on a tray on the floor. I used to colour-in paper doylies or use them as stencils over paper. How successful my attempts were I can't say without prejudice, but it kept me happily occupied for hours. Years later my daughter and I spent days on end making flower designs using a compass to create the petals and then coloured them in as took our fancy. For a considerable number of years these were the basis for the staple home-made birthday card from our family. When a small girl explained that she couldn't complete her homework (not that it was a burden I'd intended) as she didn't have any art equipment at home I was aghast, but I thought it must be an isolated case. Sadly, not so.

I suppose that compared to the sophisticated graphics on computer games pencil crayons do seem a bit out of date, but I think that it's a sorry state and I'm not sure that it really represents progress. The other problem was that these kids never really have the time to do their piano practice and so they certainly haven't got time to do any unnecessary colouring sheets. The problem with so many activities is that it prevents any one thing being done really well. If every minute is allocated then when is there time for the child to do any piano practice? Or when can they practise their ballet exercises? Or when can they put their swimming lessons to good use and actually "go swimming?" I do wonder if some parents choose for their children to take music lessons merely to provide a topic of conversation whilst waiting in the ballet changing rooms? At least then there is the scope to discuss what colour the music room colour scheme will follow when they next redecorate.

Gratefully yours, x

Dear Reader,

It is true that the genre of classical music can seem elitist and exclusive, but this really isn't the case at all. If anybody has the desire or even the merest inclination to 'join the club' it really is open to all. I appreciate that not everybody is able to purchase or learn particular instruments, although for the really keen there are ways and means. The electronic keyboard is a relatively inexpensive and space saving instrument, although it's not a genuine alternative to the piano - but it's certainly enough to get you started. I suppose it all depends upon what your priorities are. For decades I practised on an inferior (and quite ugly) piano which was "free to a good home." It was just about in tune with itself but could never be tuned to concert pitch. Being straight-strung meant a lesser string length (as opposed to over-strung which gave a greater string length) which results in a poorer sound quality and the strings would have snapped if too much pressure was exerted on them in an attempt to reach A = 440.

There are those who *won't* purchase a piano (rather than *can't* purchase a piano) because it would interfere with the interior design of the home. I do have a delicate sense of artistic taste within the home but I appreciate that function over form also has its place - especially when making room for a piano. As students my husband and I lived in a tiny flat but we still managed to squeeze an old piano into the lounge. You can imagine that the removal men were thrilled by my persistence in having a piano delivered up two flights of stairs. I have had pupils pay for piano lessons with no instrument to practise on after getting rid of a perfectly good piano because it clashed with their new decor and not replacing it for more than two years - yet they kept on paying for piano lessons throughout this time.

If the piano, or even the keyboard, isn't particularly your instrument of choice there are other, more portable instruments to choose from, but perhaps aspects of lack of practice time or finance for tuition is inhibiting. There's no doubt that learning to play an instrument requires a significant amount of time and effort. However, we all possess an instrument that is free and instantly accessible - our voice. If ever you feel the inclination to extend your vocal activities from merely singing in the shower there are plenty of amateur choirs to suit all tastes. Some are more formal than others and this is reflected in the style and difficulty of the music rehearsed. I love singing in an unusually large amateur choir of about 120 members, which means that we can attempt some quite serious musical works and can also sing with a full orchestra (as often as budget allows - they're expensive) without sounding imbalanced. It's hard to describe the joy of participating in such hefty works as Vaughan William's "Sea Symphony," Carl Orff's "Carmina Burana" and Vivaldi's "Gloria", as well as various Requiems and other standard fayre.

Each choir has its own audition requirements to suit the ability of the projected membership. Some choirs adopt a policy of unrestricted access but you do have to realise that this will reflect in the quality of the output of the choir. You mustn't see this auditioning process as some dreadful test, it's more of an opportunity for the conductor to gauge where best to place you in the choir. Even so, make sure that you have a modest idea of your own ability...

Rehearsal began as usual and Audley, our conductor, began the usual rigmarole of "warm-ups." Before we even begin singing all dignity is thrown to the winds as he has us bending and twisting this way and that. Vocal cords then get the warm-up treatment as he orders us to make strange shrieking noises and yawning effects. Now we are ready for the scales and vowel exercises. By now we are all thoroughly embarrassed (although equally supple and versatile in body and voice) and so it's a matter of self preservation to avoid eye contact with your choral neighbour. As the choir began ascending and descending vowel sounds a strange whining noise appeared on the edge of hearing and gradually grew in intensity. A little confused, but as yet undaunted, Audley brought down the baton and retried the exercise. Again the same banshee sounds soared above the scales - it seemed to be coming from the front row of the basses. Admittedly we were attempting a new vocal exercise and I won't be the last one to say that, at times, the basses do miss the point (or the pitch), but this was something quite different. Abandoning the new exercise, being at a loss to discern the problem, we reverted to some tried and tested sequences but the culprit was obviously gaining confidence and the situation was getting worse. It was also being replicated in the second sopranos - on our row! By now the rehearsal was in disarray and everyone was looking around in horrified wonder trying to pin-point the instigator of the problem. Although Audley is a man of many talents, in this instance he had no idea how to discover why the rehearsal was in a shambles. We began work on the current repertoire but the situation simply got worse. We were learning a new piece which was technically very difficult and also very discordant (by design). It was impossible to tell which were the right 'wrong' notes - which clashes were composed and which were improvised. The culprits, it transpired, were two strangers who had launched themselves upon us and seemed to be having a great time.

During the interval it would have been helpful to have had a bit of a chat with the two new prospective members (not that they'd ever be allowed to officially join) but this was impossible as they spent the entire break locked in each other's arms in a passionate embrace. The situation really needed to be dealt with but nobody seemed willing to take the matter into their own hands and nobody knew quite what to do. Too long was spent deliberating the problem and the conductor was back at his stand ready to plunge into the rehearsal again - such a brave man. Hurried whispering amongst various committee members suggested that the problem be investigated further by catching the newcomers at the end of the rehearsal. Such plans were again thwarted as the couple left a quarter of an hour before the rehearsal ended. Fifteen minutes wasn't long to make progress with the piece but we did what we could, there'd always be next week.

Early the next Tuesday the required committee members drove to our rehearsal venue, to put out the chairs, only to find the passionate pair keeping themselves busy until somebody opened the door. Polite conversation followed and tentative enquiries were made. It was made clear that a strict audition process was needed in order to become a member of the choir. Hearty acknowledgement indicated that such a process would not daunt them and another chaotic rehearsal ensued. Lack of any sense of pitch was, of course, a serious issue but the main problem was that neither the bass nor the soprano were bothering to look at the music books which had been loaned to them. Totally oblivious to the mayhem that they were creating, they were having a jolly good sing-song! Caught up in the joy of choral singing they were giving vent to the most unguarded rapture of word and voice that I have ever witnessed. They were making their own sounds, their own words and were totally indiscriminate in terms of pitch and volume. It was a wonder to behold. Somehow or other the conductor made the best of a bad business. In our foolishness we thought that protocol would take its course and this would be the last rehearsal that could be affected by such a racket.

During the interval the couple managed to keep away from each other's lips and chatted among the voice groupings. We started to smell a rat when the soprano told me that she'd come to the choir because she liked being with old people. (I took great exception to that.) She then asked Maggie (who is an OAP) if she liked singing karaoke. It was patiently explained that they would need to see the conductor at the end of the rehearsal and audition before they could continue. (False hope - but what can you do?)

Our hopes were dashed once more when they scuttled away fifteen minutes before the end of rehearsal - this couldn't happen again! A vigilant tenor noticed that a taxi had pulled up to take them away and ran out of rehearsal to ask where they were going. It was discovered that, as a matter of economy, they'd walked almost eight miles to get to rehearsal but were taking a cab home. There would be no rehearsal next week as it was a school holiday but matters obviously needed taking into hand. The Chairman was forced to step up to the plate and track them down to clarify the situation. It was quite sad really as there were obviously other learning difficulties here, but our choir really wasn't the place for them. This may sound discriminatory, but that's the point - you are discriminated, not only by your ability, but also by your voice range. During the audition process you are allocated a seat according to your vocal range. I am discriminated from sitting in the alto section, even though I'd like to sit next to my friend there. Sadly it also follows that someone who is utterly tone deaf is discriminated from joining the choir - Vivaldi didn't write for dissonant divas.

The audition process for the choir I belong to falls somewhere in the middle of the spectrum. New members do need to pass an audition merely to ascertain that they aren't totally tone-deaf and to be properly allocated to soprano, alto, tenor or bass. Music is a very equal opportunities arena and we show no preference to either male or female (though we would like some more tenors and basses, please).

Some years ago I remember a young man, in his early twenties, who after auditioning with a very high voice was discovered to be a countertenor and asked to sit next to a group of old women. I'm surprised he lasted as many months as he did, but I guess his days were always numbered.

It isn't a prerequisite to be able to read music to join our choir - but it helps. Many members learn their parts simply by piggy-backing on their neighbour's ability during rehearsal and then by listening to the CD at home. After repeated years of rehearsal they must surely pick up some note reading skills. Open access does have its pitfalls though as it can encourage an "easy-come, easy-go" attitude. I know for a fact that certain members live out a dichotomy of hypocrisy. On the very front row of the sopranos is a teacher with the reputation for being a strict disciplinarian and having a fiery temper. Remarkably she sits during rehearsal playing games on her mobile phone! Bank managers and solicitors talk openly whilst the conductor is speaking and most slouch in their seats with their music covering their face so that they can neither breathe properly nor see the conductor. It's enough to make one's blood boil!

Gratefully yours, x

Dear Reader,

Although the piano has eighty eight notes and the flute has thirty seven notes (unless you buy a supremely expensive extension joint and have an out-of-this-world technique to afford you a few extra semitones) all a musician really needs is eight notes. Just a basic octave covers the major scale which forms the basis for our Western tonal system.

As a teenager it seemed good to me to explore the world of campanology and so, each Tuesday evening, I climbed the precariously winding steps up the local church tower and held on tightly to bell number four. Ranging from lightest to heaviest bell numbers four and five were allocated "beginner bells." Bell numbers one to three were much too light and frisky and numbers six to eight were deemed to heavy for a slip of a girl like me. (I don't think I'd have that worry now, alas.) Yet again I find in myself a penchant for music making in broom cupboard-esque establishments. The church was only a small village affair and the tower could be described as "cosy" by an exuberantly optimistic estate agent. Standing shoulder to shoulder in a cramped circle music is made (potentially) by the pulling of ropes in succession of varied combinations. It sounds simple but is in fact quite terrifying. If you pull too hard, or before the rope has properly uncoiled, you stand to break the stay on which the bell itself is hung. There's a rhythm to the process quite apart from the musical aspect. The leader of our group was an elderly gent, named Stanley, and I'm ashamed to say that he had cause to climb the rickety ladder into the bell loft with a hammer and nails more than once on my account. It's always a bonus to keep a tight hold the the rope too. This was an objective that I didn't always grasp (rather like the rope), thus sending Stanley up the ladder yet again.

Bell ringing is really mathematical. If you progress into the higher echelons you must memorise long mathematical progressions to translate into melodies such as Plain Hunt. This is termed "Change Ringing" as it describes the bells "changing" places. Plain Hunt Doubles uses six bells, the sixth bell is the tenor bell and ends each phrase or sequence. Plain Hunt Doubles follows this sequence:

$$123456$$
$$214356$$
$$241356$$
$$425136$$
$$452316$$
$$543216$$
$$351426$$
$$315246$$
$$132546$$
$$123456$$

It is more easily remembered (so I'm led to believe) by drawing a visual line to trace your individual bell. I'm afraid that this was beyond my mental mathematical skills at the time and I restricted myself to "Call Changes." Here the conductor dictates the pattern and calls the order. Numbers are shouted in pairs so that each ringer is directed regarding which bell to follow. For example, "three to seven" would mean that ringer number three would pull their downward stroke directly after the ringer of bell number seven has pulled down.

Call Change ringing should be plain sailing, but in our group there was an awkward problem that threw a spanner in the works. As Stanley was directing the pattern he'd begin to say, 'One to four (or five) … Eight to six (or seven).' However, he'd get past the first two words and then the trouble would start. You see, Stanley had a particularly bad stammer which left us on pins. ''One to f..f..f..f..' he'd begin and it would take some time before it was clear whether bell number four or five was up next. Similarly he would call, 'Eight to s..s..s..s..' and all would be chaos. By the time we'd gathered if number six or seven was to follow it was too late and everybody had lost the momentum of their bell.The end result was an aural rendition of the whole bell tower collapsing in on top of itself All the notes had stacked up in the waiting queue and then rushed on in together when the ropes simply had to come down. You have to maintain the momentum of the rope. If you pause for too long the music comes to a standstill, but mores seriously you risk jolting the bell off it's stay. Sometimes one of the more experienced ringers would take an educated guess about what was to come next and give a nod to the waiting ringers in attempt to keep musical flow, but it was a serious thing to usurp Stanley's authority and nobody dared try this too often.

Poor Stanley! It simply wasn't the job for him despite his experience and ability. As far as I could gather it was the same old story, Stanley had been there for years and had taken his position by some form of osmosis and that was how it stayed. Nobody had the heart to broach the topic and if Stanley was aware of the chaos he caused he didn't seem too concerned. At least this wasn't an issue when we were change ringing and here harmony reigned (unless I'd forgotten the sequence again).

I love the cultural overtones of the practice of campanology, it's so jolly British! What could be better, on a sultry summer evening (should we ever get one) than sitting in the garden, sipping Prosecco and listening to bell practice? (This of course presumes that Stanley isn't calling the changes.) It annoys me that policy has become so ridiculous that a special licence has to be prearranged, otherwise you could get slapped with a Noise Abatement Order. Although, on reflection, if Stanley was directing perhaps it makes sense.

I can't think why my friend and I first got the idea to go bell ringing into our heads. I have a sneaking suspicion that a couple of young, male members may have been the initial motivation. I'm quite positive that our joining the group had absolutely nothing to do with the fact that they left soon after our arrival. Nevertheless, we stayed on and so our ultimate objective must have been intrinsically pure in heart.

Gratefully yours, x

Dear Reader,

I've noticed over recent years that the trend for school orchestras is diminishing, but this doesn't necessarily infer that quality is also always diminished. A smaller size can often mean that all sorts of funky variations can be attempted. I know of a school that has its own jazz orchestra which performs top notch music at functions all over, including venues as far off as Italy. When I was a student my school orchestra was a traditional orchestra with quite a large number of musicians and boasted unusually large numbers of oboes, bassoons, cellos and violas as well as the usual violins, flute and clarinets. However, the only place we ever ventured to was to Barlaston, North Staffordshire. Ah, me. They were innocent days (and if they weren't it went over my head). The highlight of each day was a walk in the grounds and an excursion to the local sweet shop rather than the expected unofficial attempt at the off-licence (not that we'd a chance of getting served, even if we'd tried). The wonder is that we never even thought to attempt it. The height of my rebellion was to once hide some cans of light beer inside the cabinet of my piano because my friend had bought them but didn't like the taste and didn't know how to get rid of them quickly without her mum smelling them from the drains. (We didn't think of pouring them down the loo and following it with successive flushings.) Nevertheless, we hugely enjoyed our annual orchestral holiday and each year it was long awaited. I still remember with fondness breaking off for sectional practice. About half a dozen of us were seated in a circle inside the huge bay window of the vast Georgian house, rehearsing an arrangement of Mozart's 'Eine Kleine Nachtmusik' whilst looking out into the gorgeous park of Rhododendrons and Azaleas (not that I knew their names back then). It cultivated a deep and genuine love for the beauty of classical music and it encouraged a true appreciation for participating in live musical performance. It also instilled the discipline needed to practice and to aspire to better things. There's no pleasure quite like it and I'm grateful for those days. It shaped my character more than I could have imagined.

In reality the music teachers demonstrated amazing creativity in disguising five long days of toil and hard work in the context of a holiday. Each day we'd be up at half past seven, so as to be breakfasted and seated at our music stands by nine o'clock sharp. Other than a couple of fifteen minute breaks we'd be rehearsing solidly until lunch at one o'clock. Rehearsal would begin again at two o'clock and would continue until six o'clock with just one more short break at about four o'clock. The sense of satisfaction and camaraderie was incredible. Spending five days together engrossed in the common goal of getting to grips with Haydn and Mozart, or even the Star Wars film score was pure bliss. The string players must have had fingertips of leather and I know that the brass players found their embouchure collapsing just as break time was approaching. I think the tutors must have done extensive research to determine the breaking point of a young musician and timed the breaks to fall just within these limits. We wind players had it relatively easy, although I was ready enough for juice and biscuits. The only real break from this gruelling schedule was the daily lunchtime walk, (I can assure you that we genuinely needed some fresh air and a sugar boost) and one afternoon off-timetable in the middle of the week, for jolly organised activities. Looking back I suppose that the purpose of the activities organised during this prescribed break from rehearsal were "Team Building," although you'd have thought that rehearsing as an orchestra for a whole week was teamwork enough.

I've already confessed to you, dear reader, that musicians can sometimes display a startling naïvety and ignorance of the obvious and some of the activities organised for this afternoon off perfectly display this "out of touch" mentality. On our afternoon off from rehearsal two hours following on from lunch were allocated to a 'Duet Walk' in which orchestral members were paired off to walk in the extensive grounds, chat and generally get to know each other. The organisers had attempted a flash of creativity in keeping the titles of the activities music related but they'd missed an important factor, especially when you consider that this was a group of teenagers. In an attempt to be objective and to pair off students without bias names were picked out of a "hat." More specifically, names were actually picked out of two "hats." One contained boys names and the other the names of the girls of the orchestra. Fortunately (or unfortunately, depending upon your point of view) there was an unusually proportionate number of boys and girls and so the Duet Walk made the perfect blind-date system, with only the occasional awkward trio. I know that a certain amount of bartering went on behind the teacher's backs and many name tickets were exchanged for a token bag of sweets as a matter of course.

Maybe the teachers weren't as naïve as we thought. Perhaps they knew very well what they were about as I'm quite sure that a good number of budding romances began by means of a combination of the lottery system and a dash of bartering here and there, ensuring that the musical inclination stayed "in the family" so to speak. It's highly likely that second and third generation brass, wind and string players are a direct result of the "Duet Walk" and a surreptitious bag of sweets. I guess that musicians might not be quite as stupid as they at first might seem. I'm afraid that such efforts were wasted on me. At the time I obviously wasn't ready for romance. One year I remember that I was paired up with the school heart-throb and I heard all the other girls sigh with despair as his name was matched to mine (not that I cared). Once outside I experienced an uncommon surge of popularity as I negotiated to swap tickets with the highest bidder. I suspect that I got a hefty bag of sweets and a couple of cans of Cola for that exchange. My disinterest must have been genuine because, in my early Twenties, I broke rank completely and married an art student. I guess you can't win them all!

Gratefully yours, x

Dear Reader,

My heart sinks into my boots when a student walks into a lesson sporting tell-tale bandages on their hands, sporting being the operative word here. I know that I'm in for at least a few weeks of single-handed combat at the piano. If it's a flute student then we're totally scuppered and restricted to music theory, but with no writing. Although I was "that kid" who never got picked for the sport's team (and was thankful to be overlooked) I realise that not everybody conforms to this stereotype. Many of my younger pupils are actively involved in numerous sports and Terry, my long-standing adult pupil, is busier playing football and squash than I ever was with a family of three children. Karyn is one of my most able students and she also represents her school for both cross-country running and netball. It's not unusual for her to turn up to her lesson wearing her PE kit and a ruddy complexion after just finishing a league tournament and a hasty pack of sandwiches before she turns her thoughts to music.

Netball and basketball are the worst possible sports that a musician can play. Usually injuries sustained in other sports aren't quite so detrimental to musical performance. For example, leg injuries sustained in football skirmishes, or that specific tight ball of bruising from the squash ball are lamentable but don't particularly impinge upon woodwind or piano performance. I suppose that facial injuries from a rugby scrum could have a damaging effect on a flute player's embouchure, but it's a combination that I've never encountered. Unfortunately, lessons are constantly disrupted by numerous permutations of strapped fingers after a misjudged attempt at catching a netball or basketball. They are heavy things and fingers have a tendency to succumb to the physics of force and motion and so they bend, or snap backwards after a hefty throw. They also take a long time to mend!

Megan is a fine example of breaking the boundaries of stereotyping. When she began high school she was something of a lost cause and was known as a trouble maker. Somehow her hands found their way to a piano keyboard and she hasn't looked back since. She is now a model student. She's hardworking, has a lovely attitude and is a very capable musician. I'm duty bound to add that her salvation can't solely be attributed to her affinity with the piano as she took up boxing and running at about the same time. No doubt these activities go a good way towards channelling her previously pent-up aggression, leaving her becalmed spirit to express itself through the beautiful music she practices so diligently. I have no qualms about any conflict of interests because her legs, which run so capably, are no concern of mine and although boxing does involve her hands the size of the gloves she wears removes any lingering doubt.

A less regular source of consternation, but still a matter of concern, is the pastime of skiing. Although not usually a weekly activity it holds the potential to create an annual disturbance, usually just around exam time. It seems that if you fall when skiing simply anything can break. As I've already mentioned, broken legs don't intrinsically concern me. Fingers however are a constant source of worry and have often meant a cancelled exam over the years. Even if the fall was months before the exam date the resultant lack of practice and preparation means that the exam material won't be ready in time. The most extreme case I've come across was a skiing accident which resulted in a broken collarbone just weeks before a pre-paid flute exam. The most obvious course of action was to cancel the exam and the student would have to forego the exam fee, which wasn't burdensome. Either the family was exceptionally thrifty or they had a hardy, disciplined approach to life, as the parents insisted that everything should proceed as planned. The poor lad had to practise holding his flute with his right elbow resting on a bookcase shelf to take the strain from his painful collarbone. His well-meaning mother was also unfortunately rather overbearing and for the first week insisted that she herself should support his arm as he played. What fifteen year old wants his mother clutching at his elbow and peering over his shoulder for half an hour at a time? I can't imagine that she forbore to comment during this time either - I'm not convinced that she could actually keep quiet for that amount of time. Attempting a little diplomacy it was suggested that the student himself would best know what was most comfortable and so as not to cause further damage with inappropriate pressure being unwittingly exerted on the injury the bookcase took over the job. A happy byproduct was that any helpful comments that the mother might have felt incumbent to bestow had to wait their turn.

My husband, David, used to participate in all sorts of extreme sports. He'd go rock climbing with no ropes, which I'm convinced is why he now has Raynauds in his fingers. He also ran marathons, which is why his knees are now shot to pieces. I'm pleased to report that, because I've spent years just sitting playing the piano, all of my joints are just fine.

Gratefully yours, x

Dear Reader,

I know that I've already confided in you that I get nervous before I start teaching each day so it's no surprise that the twenty minutes before there is the first knock at the door can see me nipping to the loo about three times. I guess that it's just a very diluted version of stage fright. (Please excuse the inadvertent reference to water again there.) Perhaps it's a good sign, really. Maybe the day that I don't get a touch of the jitters is the day that I know to pack in: Never rest on your laurels, there's always something new to learn. It's no wonder that people who work in the arts can often end up a "bit strange." What can you expect from a group of people who have to live on their nerves for their daily bread? I guess that it's part of the job and it's something that you learn to deal with. Performance nerves are particularly tricky to deal with, but there are coping mechanisms that you can learn to adopt to help alleviate this to a degree. The jitters will never fully leave you but if you accept them as a matter of course it does take a little of the fraughtness out of the situation. I have a mental lecture prepared that I've developed over the years and when the nerves start to kick in the lecture is triggered and I take myself through each bullet point:

- Nerves are good! A dose of adrenalin adds an edge of creativity to your performance. No nerves makes for a dull rendition.

- There's no real foundation for such nervousness. At this point I check off the preparation that has taken place. If I've spent sufficient time in practice I can reassure myself that my fingers already know what they're doing. Muscle memory can take over and my brain needn't get too involved. Here, however, is a caveat. If I've not practised and I know that the reason I'm on edge is because I'm not sufficiently prepared then I deserve to be nervous. It's a just punishment. If this is the case (which it might well be) then my little homily divides into a sub-clause:

- You've not practised and you deserve to be nervous, but there's nothing new in this. (Ain't that the truth!) You've been here before and you've pulled it off (by the seat of your pants). Let this be a lesson to you. I now begin promising myself that I'll turn over a new leaf and vow to always practise diligently henceforth. Once I've got through the current performance crisis (again) I'll lapse into inactivity for a while, until the next crisis.

I know of only two people who genuinely never get nervous, and they practise simply all of the time. Because they live and breathe music every waking minute another performance is all in a day's work to them. Both of these examples are male and I suspect that the X chromosome predominantly carries the "nervousness gene." As such, this explains why we women often get so nervous - we have a double helping to cope with.

I'm sure that a large part of my nervousness arises from the fact that I'm constantly lurching between two worlds - the domestic and the musical. Those friends of mine that don't have families spend their time in uninterrupted practise and musical application whereas I'm constantly jumping ship, between music and domestics, and this takes a good deal of mental adjustment. Two minutes before a pupil knocks at the door I'm just dashing to the washing machine to swap loads. If I have a gap between pupils I've an eye on the clock wondering if I should put the oven on to pre-heat so that I have supper ready for us all by half past eight. If I'm not teaching and have a morning at home I'll plan to do some music practise before my pupils arrive. I'll start a quick tidy so that the house is ready to receive visitors, then I'll walk the dog (who is getting older and much, much slower) and then it's time to prepare some lunch for us all (which can be for between two and seven people on an irregular and ever changing basis). I'll then get side-tracked with some laundry and before I know it I've missed my chance and my pupils are due. No wonder it takes me a moment to figure out which end of the flute to blow down. David always tells me to practise first thing in a morning and we can pull the domestics together between us as and when we can each day. I can't adjust to this as I hate working amongst clutter and my attitude isn't bohemian enough to have pupils and parents surrounded by my family's paraphernalia - though I gather it's 'arty' to do so. I've managed on my wits for the last twenty years so I suppose I can manage a little bit longer.

When new pupils begin to take lessons they are a veritable bag of nerves. It's no wonder that they are nervous when you consider that, in essence, those first lessons are a performance test (or so it could feel to the pupil) that they have absolutely no means of preparing for, thus creating a maximum potential for the jitters. My heart does go out to them and I work really hard to put them at their ease. I reassure new students that music lessons are supposed to sound nasty and if they didn't make any mistakes they wouldn't need to take lessons and we'd have to swap seats.

I used to cry before my piano lessons - even as an adult! I also know that this was because I knew full well that I hadn't practised what I should have and no doubt some exam was looming and I'd left everything to the last minute. At this juncture I really must explain that all of my teachers were really nice and would be mortified to learn that I'd got myself into such a tizzy. They'd also laugh at me heartily now and tell me that I was an idiot and it was my own fault. Ah, such wisdom!

No doubt there is much potential for research into the "nervousness qualities" of the X chromosome. Maybe I should apply for a grant. Although, on reflection I'm not sure that this is robust enough to stand up to empirical testing. The most anxious students are always beginner adult males and the older they are the more nervous they appear to be. It must be quite an ordeal for a grown man to sit himself next to a complete stranger and feel like an imbecile until they find their fingers. The situation is the same for all beginners but adult males do seem to feel it more acutely. Their knees are continually bouncing (if not literally knocking) as their nervous tension finds physical expression. Their speech is halting, if not entirely non-existent and their hands shake violently as they try and play. Outside of the music room they probably manage to maintain a façade of cool confidence in new situations but at the piano all such masks are torn asunder. It usually takes a couple of months for them to get to know me and feel fully at ease. There's definitely a research grant in this somewhere with any findings to be used to develop new methods of the cruelest psychological torture.

Gratefully yours, x

Dear Reader,

Broom cupboards are obviously my natural habitat. I've consistently shown a propensity to take up residence in various cupboard style abodes for over twenty years. I obviously feel at home in such places. It's a typical case of "The Lesser Spotted Piano Teacher" which may be found, if you're lucky, in secluded places throughout Great Britain. If you sit very still and are very quiet you may actually see one.

I began my married life in a broom cupboard-esque flat. David and I got married as students, figuring that there was no good time for a free-lance artist and musician to settle down so we may as well face what comes together. If we'd waited for financial security we'd still be waiting more than twenty years later. We set up home in a little flat above my brother-in-law's business. More accurately it was split between ground level and the first floor which branched off from a narrow winding staircase. A small kitchenette doubled as an entrance / reception room from which a spiral staircase led to the upper living quarters. At the top of the stairs the door straight ahead led to the main living room, which also served as a dining room and art studio - even I couldn't get a piano up there. The sofa acted as a room divider, sectioning off a massive cast iron AO drawing table which also provided us with a dining table if we cleared all the paper away. David had salvaged this monstrosity from a British Telecom office clearance and the one point in its favour was that it was durable. Opposite the single, dilapidated sofa was "Book Case Corner" (my attempt at sectioning off a study area and mini library). This completed the furnishings in the lounge. We had no TV, nor have had for most of our married life. A well meaning relative thought that it was against our human rights not to own a TV and gave us a portable black and white TV set, but watching the snooker championship on a fifteen inch, monochrome screen isn't as engaging as it might seem and we quietly secreted it away.

I guess that for much of our time we were busy working or I just enjoyed pottering about playing house. I did have my flute that I could play there but I'd had to keep my piano at my parent's house so I'd visit them to do some piano practice or to teach the few pupils I'd got at the time. I'd usually beg a hot meal at the same time. For many hours David would be working at his drawing table and I'd sit, wrapped in blankets, doing some sewing or reading a book. One evening we'd shared a bottle of wine and David thought that it would be a good idea to paint my portrait and so, between sips, a hasty oil sketch was executed. At the end of the evening we looked with pleasure at the canvas resting on top of Book Case Corner and went to sleep satisfied with our evening. Hindsight is a wonderful science and we now know (with the wisdom of age and experience) that alcohol and portraiture do not make a happy partnership. The next morning I skipped happily into the lounge and, on seeing the bedaubed canvas, broke down in tears when I thought that I really might look like what was depicted in oils. I'm still haunted by that canvas because I can't ever remember us throwing it away. We soon cried with laughter, once the shock had worn off, but I've a lingering worry that one day it will once again rear its ugly head (quite literally) and I'll lose my sense of humour again.

There was a small window in the lounge (an unusual luxury in my experience of broom cupboards) which overlooked a main roundabout on a busy major junction. This view wasn't as bad as it sounds as the town was a Britain in Bloom prize winner. At the centre of the roundabout several subways converged and a floral centre piece made for quite a pretty view. We referred to this as our garden and during the summer we would sometimes join the resident tramps and eat a picnic there.

We had a very happy start to our married life in that pokey little flat. Perhaps that explains why I'm happy to continue to exist in a variety of broom cupboards years after our domestic residence has improved and enlarged. I obviously find a sense of womb-like security when working in various closeted practice rooms. If you stay very still you might observe similar specimens of the Lesser Spotted Peripatetic Music Tutor in their natural habitat. Be very careful not to alarm them.

Gratefully yours, x

Dear Reader,

I know that even the best of us can be a shade condescending but I have to agree that musicians have the greatest potential to be snobbish and we often use that potential to the full. Classical musicians have a deep-seated prejudicial snobbery that follows a complex system of hierarchy which they give full vent to. Popular musicians tend to nurse an inverted form of individualised snobbery for anybody who isn't themselves. You must forgive such rank generalisation but it's more accurate than you'd be comfortable to believe.

Flautists have the reputation for being gossipy and spiteful and I'd like to think that I disprove this typecast. You'd have to ask around. Within the keyboard world there's a pecking order which is finely tuned (if you'll excuse the pun) which divides and then subdivides between the organ and piano genres. At the very bottom of the tree is the amateur keyboard player who reads only right hand treble clef and left hand chord symbols. I realise that there are some amazingly talented popular keyboard players, but they stand outside of this ranking system. I give full warning, here and now, to any hopefuls that may want to join the clique: If you ever press the auto arpeggio button or the auto chord function all that you will experience is a cold wind and many proverbial backs as we all walk away. Everybody has to start somewhere but the second that you press that button our welcome is revoked. Sharing last place is the electronic organist. This is not to be confused with the elite pipe organist (or the electric/digital counterpart) at the very top of the tree. The distinction here is very specific; if you play with your right hand on the top manual reading treble clef, follow chord symbols with your left hand on the second manual and only the toes of your left foot hover dubiously over one octave of pedals, the only way is up. However, although we encourage you to practice hard and extend these skills, if you just touch the auto chord or arpeggio button you can wave good bye - although nobody will be looking. If you use the rhythm function we might shake our heads a little but we will be impressed if you can stay in time. If you can't, please leave the swing beat turned off. Within both genres of organ playing you'll be branded as a heretic if you take your shoes off to play the pedals. I would say that this is regardless of whether you're an electronic organ player or a pipe organist but I can honestly say that I have never, ever known - in the entirety of my career - of a pipe organist who would do such a thing.

I'm confused to know to which part of the hierarchy Rosemarie rightly belongs. She's been coming to me for piano lessons for some years now and is a very able student who shows great potential as a musician. She practises diligently and plays sensitively but stubbornly insists upon taking her shoes and socks off to employ the piano sustain pedal. This stereotypically makes her rightful position in the ranks null and void. She also persists in working the action of the pedal via her knee joint, rather than her ankle. The result a very messy affair in which her knee spasmodically jerks up and down while her prehensile toes grip the metal pedal.

Musically the correct effect is achieved but the atmosphere is totally sabotaged. There's always one!

You may be shocked to learn that such a pecking order exists (albeit an unspoken one) but that's just the way it is. I'm sure that sitting at a different desk there is a different author penning a similar text on the way of things in the realm of office politics and I'm intrigued to know how they've sufficient gaps in their day to write to their own dear and valued reader. Maybe ledgers go missing and files fail to arrive as frequently as music pupils. Perhaps there's a Bermuda Triangle somewhere out there that is quickly filling up with truant musicians who are having to fill their half hour slot with homeless invoices and receipts that need help in pairing off. I'll bet they wish they'd turned up to their lesson instead now they're having to play matchmaker to hopeless and needy cases of paperwork!

It's only fair to say that the system works. I myself started with an enforced stay in the electronic organ world (although you may rest assured that I NEVER took my shoes off) and the tangible sense of shame urged me to practise and practise so as to move up the ranks and shake off the humiliation. It motivated me to earn my place in the gathering of serious musicians, if only on the bottom rung. If you aspire to join in and move up all you have to do is apply yourself. We'll even give you a helping hand - that's why I'm here. Although my simply being here isn't enough to secure you a place in the golden throng, you do have to actually turn up to your lesson to do some work, and you do need to do some work under your own steam between lessons. The fact that I'm writing to you again, my dear reader, is testimony to the fact that there are those whose hearts have hardened to their situation. Either that or they harbour the misapprehension that they've already made it!

Gratefully yours, x

Dear Reader,

After decades of entertaining pupils of all shapes and varieties I've developed something of a sixth sense. It's a common trait in all established music tutors. My friend, Mae, reckons that she can smell trouble from the briefest telephone enquiry and can quickly discern that her books are quite full at the moment despite the fact that the enquiry is the direct result of a recent advertisement for pupils. She taught me well and I now possess something of her powers. There are many tell-tale signs which, although quite innocent in isolation, once combined together signal impending doom. Learning to discern the signs is rather more art than science, although some of the earliest harbingers of trouble are quite simple. Once your attention is aroused you just have to follow the verbal trail of bread crumbs and adjust as the path unfolds. There are certain standard enquiry openings that suggest calamity lies ahead:

'I won't ever make her practise. I'll just let her play what she wants to play, when she chooses.'

This is a sure sign of lurking doom. If I only ever played when I felt like it I'd still be on "Three Blind Mice." I never much fancied learning to do maths. If I'd been left to my own devices I'd now be blissfully unaware of what fees were actually due or being paid. Fortunately my parents and teachers forced me learn to how to add up, so it's thanks to them that I won't now get "ripped off." I still say that I'd rather have stayed sitting in front of "The Clangers" all night.

Another classic signal of impending disaster is,

"I don't want to learn any scales or stuff like that, I just want to be able to improvise and play jazzy stuff."

Well, now then. It seems that we are locked in something of an impasse before we've even met. Silly me, I'll just go and find my pot of Magic Dust and that'll sort it. I won't be long. It must be here somewhere...

The classic one-liner that endures throughout the mists of time is,

"I'm not buying an instrument until I see if he's got "it." If he takes to it then we'll think about it."

Such a relationship is ill-fated from square one. In the first instance I suspect that it's socially taboo to dare to ask precisely what "it" actually is. I have a sneaky feeling that I'll be searching for that pot of Magic Dust again (though I never can seem to lay my hands on it). Putting "it" to one side, I hardly dare ask how anyone will ever "take" to music if they only get to play for a maximum of thirty minutes per week. I was obviously a very slow witted student as I foolishly spent the bloom of my youth playing scales and Schumann for hours on end before I could get "it." Perhaps it's only the feeble few who need to practise, or to work and re-work small sections of notes and fingering. I guess that we'd better swap seats while they liberally sprinkle me with the fairy dust that they obviously own. I still can't find my pot.

I've mentioned before that it may not be feasible for everyone to purchase a full sized acoustic piano and it appears that not many are willing to accommodate a "free to a good home" one for aesthetic purposes, but you do need to show a modicum of good intent. A keyboard will do for starters at least. This dilemma is particularly prevalent in would-be piano students, but it isn't wholly exclusive to the keyboard genre. I regret to inform you that I have experienced enquiries for flute lessons when the potential pupil doesn't own their own flute. The audacity of a complete stranger thinking that they can man-handle my open-holed flute (presuming that their finger shape will actually cover the keys, which is an anatomical lottery outside of anyone's control) is bad enough. Take the process a logical step further and consider the audacity of presuming to spit into my solid silver lip plate before handing it back to me to demonstrate the next point (which is a bacterial lottery that I am fully in control of!) They've a wealth of musical disappointment stacking up on the not too distant horizon, I can sense it. Learning the embouchure and diaphragm control to actually sound a note on the flute can take some getting used to. How can anybody expect to achieve any progress with only ad-hoc access to somebody else's flute (though certainly not mine) once a week? It's beyond comprehension! As you can imagine, such phone calls are of very short duration.

Over time my powers of psychoanalysis have developed further than these brief forays into potential pupil divination and I have honed the ability to assess the personality type of a student by interpreting their performance style. Again this is a subtle art and, although I'm rarely wrong, there are times when an unexpected factor skews the hypothesis. Confidence is always a huge bonus when playing any instrument and a more gregarious personality will happily bash away at their music with little regard for my long term hearing and with absolutely no regard whatsoever for any wrong notes. This isn't necessarily a bad thing - oversensitivity to playing wrong notes can be really disabling to a student's progress. The main issue here is when it's a case of misplaced confidence. Tammy has oodles of confidence and attacks the keyboard with relish, it's just a pity that she has no perception (or no concern) about where she actually places her fingers. This is a general character type and they're often really pleasant people - they just don't listen. Such a temperament often goes hand in hand with an inflated sense of their own ability, and at the same time as ignoring the sound their own fingers are making they often ignore the words that I speak.

It can be tricky to initially gauge a student's ability. Without wanting to put anybody to the test it's inevitable that at some point I'll have to give them a piece of music to attempt. So as to minimise embarrassment I couch finding their levels in phrases such as, "How would you feel about looking at this?" or, "Does this look much too easy?" My intent is to give them the opportunity to say something like, "No, that doesn't look easy at all." or, " I'm not sure how I'd feel about playing this music." I hope that this is better than making them feel a complete chump as they stare blankly at the music and the piano keyboard. However, this system fails with the over confident student who will tell me that they can play whatever I put in front of them but are then utterly clueless when asked to attempt the exercise.

The flip side of this situation is the pupil who is far too self effacing. Their reticence is absolutely no reflection on their ability but more an indicator of their retiring personality. This student will tend to play every piece of music pianissimo - *issimo*. This is usually paired with an insistence to play everything at a funereal pace, even after months of consistent practice. The fear of making even a small mistake robs them of what would be a musical performance, if they dared to just "go for it." Such a lack of confidence is a real inhibitor to progress. Even in an exam a student will gain much better marks for a lively and varied performance - even with some wrong notes (although the goal is always to not have too many of these). A performance of merely accurate notes, but played as a dull mathematical exercise, is lifeless and uninspiring. If only I could mash these two personality types together. The confidence of the one mixed with the application and accuracy of the other would be a perfect combination.

However, as I mentioned earlier, I have been known (on occasion) to misinterpret the stereotype - although I'm wise to the situation now. For years I'd presumed that pupils like Debbie were cautious and timid because of how quietly they played. No amount of encouragement would convince them to apply a bit of "welly" when they played. After much of the same encouragement I did what was the only sensible thing to do. I asked Debbie in a straightforward manner why she played so quietly all of the time. Her answer was as simple as it was shocking. Her piano was in the same room as the TV and her dad got cross if she played too loudly. The wonder now was that she ever played at all. Why would her father pay for lessons and then buy her a piano, to then place it next to the TV? If it was so utterly preposterous to consider turning the TV off for half an hour or so why not place the piano in the hallway - or buy an instrument that could play through earphones? Sometimes there are just no words.

Gratefully yours, x

Dear Reader,

I've thoroughly enjoyed getting to know you over these pages. I've certainly got to know myself. It is with a heavy heart that I sense a time of separation ahead of us. I hope that we will be apart for only a short space of time, but whether or not we'll meet again is outside of my control. It rather depends upon whether you were ever really there at all. Time will tell. The end of the academic year fast approaches and I know this, if not because the calendar tell me so, because the usual signs are beginning to become apparent. Attendance is more spasmodic than ever during the last couple of weeks of term. During the usual run of the mill term-time I can usually predict who will attend and when. This is another demonstration of a sixth (or seventh, or eighth) sense that I've developed over the years. Week by week the forces that dictate attendance fluctuate according to the position of the tide or the sun in the sky. It's a certain fact that a sunny evening can mean a lean time for me - we Brits must barbecue when we can. As the summer holidays approach all of these existing modes of prediction fall by the wayside and a game of chance begins. End of year concerts, plays and general timetable mayhem mean that I get to spend these last precious moments with you, dear reader. I have found, over these weeks and months, that I cherish the time that we have had together. I almost hope for unofficial breaks in my timetable which will mean that I can talk to you. It's been my guilty pleasure throughout the academic year.

An added bonus to these enforced breaks is that I'm gradually becoming acclimatised to the fact that there is another world out there, off time-table and out of the closet. In just a few days I must blink my eyes in the sunlight and look into the distant horizons that exist out of the broom cupboard. There's a whole new world out there that I must soon step into. Dare I say it? There are people other than you, dear reader, and I must embrace such potential for face-to-face friendship other than over the piano keyboard or the music stand. It's a pity that I'll have no cash to enjoy this brave new world. Such is the case for the self employed music tutor. I used to try and continue lessons over the holiday period - a body must eat. However, I soon discovered that one can only linger pointlessly at home for so long. I'd stay home to conduct an arranged lesson only to receive a call (sometimes days later) to give profuse apology and an explanation that they'd simply forgotten, being off timetable and in the holiday mood. One can hardly blame them. I now only teach a handful of adults throughout the summer. There are still some whose lives aren't dictated by the academic calendar and have no concept of a six (or seven) week break.

What will actually be the case is that I'll be unemployed for nearly two months. I'll also merely replace one timetable for another - ever was the case. As the Jewish Proverb states, "A dog returns to its vomit, so a fool repeats his foolishness." (Proverbs 26:11) The holiday provides a time to metaphorically get off my backside by actually sitting the aforementioned backside onto the piano stool for a change and actually play the darned thing myself. It's (relatively) painless for me to sit and point whilst pontificating about the benefit of repetition and practice whilst I sit at a polite distance from the instrument in question and nurse my ever present cup of tea.

No doubt I'll read "Little Women" (again) and hopefully the laundry pile will suffer unusually brisk treatment. More than likely I'll substitute actual practice for rearranging my music shelves and, whilst blowing the dust off forgotten music, I'll decide to give it a go at two o'clock in the morning.

I've been exceedingly grateful for your friendship over these last few months, dear reader, but now I'll be truly grateful to my family and friends who'll kindly draw me away from the piles of music and carefully guide me into the sunshine - should we ever get some.

Gratefully yours, x

Also Available by Sharon Bill
from Amazon in Paperback & eBook

A summer fête in rural Cheshire, organised by the Women's Institute of Mossleigh, holds the promise of an idyllic day out in the best British tradition. Everyone is enjoying the festivities until a beloved neighbour is found dead among the bins and refuse of the village hall which saddens the holiday mood. However, it is only when Beth Williams and her twin brother Detective Chief Inspector Benedict James join forces that it becomes evident that all isn't as innocent as it at first seemed.

Beth is a piano tutor and a member of the local WI. As such she has her finger on the pulse of the undercurrents of the village and is ideally placed to find all of the seemingly inconsequential domestic details which could give her brother the insight he needs. Together, if they each pool their own particular fields of expertise, they're bound to get to the bottom of the business. Sordid crime might prevail amid the pastries and preserves for a time but, in the end, the culprit will get their just desserts.

Also Available by Sharon Bill
from Amazon in Paperback & eBook

Taking your ABRSM Music Theory exam can be nerve wracking and nerves can prevent you doing your best in any exam. Good preparation and planning is always the answer to this problem. In this exam guide I give you tried and tested technique, not only how to prepare before the exam but also the best procedure for actually in the exam room.

I've been entering pupils for ABRSM Music Theory exams for nearly thirty years and it is not unusual for them to pass with DISTINCTION, some even scoring 100%!

Follow these simple steps and improve *your* chances of gaining TOP MARKS.

Coming soon by Sharon Bill
from Amazon in Paperback & eBook

Check out **Sharon's YouTube channel** for a free accompanying series of music theory tutorials. You are guided, step by step, through the ABRSM Music Theory workbooks. Each video tutorial leads you through each exercise and free to download PDF information sheets give you everything you need to know.

There are lessons explaining all aspects of music theory and practical music topics which are simply explained so as to be easily understandable in 4k.

For everything you need to help you with your ABRSM Music theory visit....
http://www.bit.ly/SharonBillYT

& in the pipeline…

Artful Designs

The second

Beth Williams Mystery

For more information about Sharon Bill's

Writing, Blog and Music Tuition &

Free PDF Downloads

www.SharonBill.com

Facebook @SharonBillPage

Twitter @SharonEBill

Instagram @sharonbill_ig

YouTube Channel showing tuition videos in 4k

http://www.bit.ly/SharonBillYT

All video & social media page links are also

available at www.SharonBill.com

Printed in Great Britain
by Amazon

41897462R00073